Building Michigan

A Tribute to Michigan's Construction Industry

The Photographic art of

Dale Fisher

EYRY OF THE EAGLE PUBLISHING

Building Michigan

Graphic Design: Tom Putters, Echo Publications, Inc.
                Royal Oak, MI

ISBN 1-891143-24-7 $60.00 retail
Library of Congress Catalog Card Number 9 781891
143243

All images in this book are available as framed photographic art in all sizes from 16" x 20"
to 38" x 48" or in murals up to eight feet long.
An extensive collection of other Open and Limited Edition
photographic art from many other locations throughout
the United States is also available. Contact the Dale
Fisher Galleries for current prices and additional information, or visit Dale's website at www.dalefisherphoto.com

Address all inquires to:
Eyry of the Eagle Publishing
Dale Fisher Galleries
1916 Norvell Road
Grass Lake, Michigan 49240
(517) 522-3705
Fax (517) 522-4665
Email: dfisher@dalefisherphoto.com
Website: www.dalefisherphoto.com

Other Books by Dale Fisher:
Detroit (Published in 1985; now out of print)
Hard Cover, 178 pages, 139 color photographs

Michigan: From the Eyry of the Eagle
(Published in 1986; now out of print)

Detroit: Visions of the Eagle; Published in 1994
Hard Cover, 176 pages, 166 full-color photographs

Ann Arbor: Visions of the Eagle; Published in 1995
Hard Cover, 192 pages, 180 full-color photographs

Dale Fisher in 1968 with his mobile photo lab and helicopter rig which he used to photograph remote sites around the United States.

About Dale Fisher

Dale Fisher sees the world as few others do – he is perhaps the only artist/photographer in the world who works exclusively from a helicopter. Born in Ann Arbor and trained in aerial reconnaissance photography by the Navy, he has been perfecting his art since 1954. Dale is truly a pioneer in his field, and will celebrate the 50th Anniversary of the Dale Fisher Galleries in 2004.

Combining artistic vision with his perspective from above, Dale transforms such subjects as freeways, construction sites, rooftops, and parked vehicles into colorful graphic patterns. Dale optimizes the perfect setting for each subject, by working with color, light and shadow, by determining sun and weather conditions, and by avoiding helicopter shadows – all while skimming over his subjects at ground speeds of up to 120 miles per hour.

Dale turned his attention to construction projects as a subject for his art when he found his eye often drawn to the unique beauty of their designs from the air. He has taken literally thousands of images of construction projects, both for this book and for contractors and construction labor unions around the State. His previous books include *Detroit; Detroit: Visions of the Eagle; Ann Arbor: Visions of the Eagle; and MICHIGAN: From the Eyry of the Eagle.* He is founder of the Michigan Center for the Photographic Arts, a mentorship program for children located on a farm near Grass Lake, and is the owner of two fine art galleries at the same location.

Thornapple River Bridges

An old man, going a lone highway,
Came at evening, cold and grey,
To a chasm, vast and deep and wide,
The old man crossed in the twilight dim —
the swollen stream was naught to him;
but he stopped when safe on the farther side,
and built a bridge to span the tide.

"Old man," said the fellow pilgrim near,
"you are wasting your strength in labor here;
your journey will end with the closing day;
you never again will pass this way,
You've crossed the chasm deep and wide,
why build you this bridge at eventide?"

The laborer lifted his old grey head,
"Good friend, in the path I have come," he said
"there follows after me today,
some youths whose feet must pass this way,
This chasm which has been naught to me,
to those young lives may a pitfall be.
They, too, must cross in the twilight dim.
Good friend, I am building this bridge for them."

—Author Unknown

Dedication

This book is respectfully dedicated
to the men and women of the
Michigan construction industry.

Introduction

DALE FISHER

A Unique Perspective

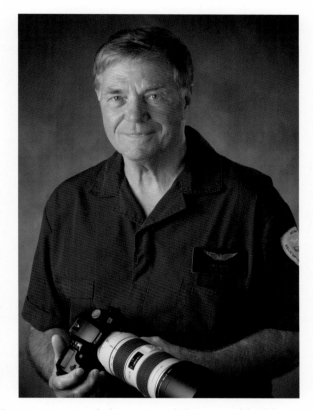

When people think of what defines beauty in Michigan, they are understandably drawn to our wonderful lakes, our majestic forests, and even our patchwork quilt of rolling farmlands all across the state. But I see beauty in something more.

Every day, we drive on roads and highways of magnificent design that we scarcely notice. We take for granted the incredible structures that we work, shop or live in, rarely thinking about the tremendous teamwork and logistics required to make these buildings a reality. Beneath the ground are complex systems of rebar, concrete, pipes, valves, cables and switches that lay beyond our ability to see, but are engineering masterpieces essential to our way of life.

These systems and structures are so integrated into our daily lives, we simply fail to recognize them. We don't comprehend the skills and dedication of thousands of Michigan's construction workers who themselves are artists of planning and design and building precision. But especially from the view of a helicopter, the magnitude of all they have done becomes incredibly clear.

The pages of this book, I hope, will help us all to see the accomplishments of Michigan's construction industry with new eyes. But there is so much more to appreciate than what can be shown in this small sampling of images. It is not only the vision of the architect and the professional management of the worksite that brings these projects to life. It is the daily toil of each individual construction worker, and the mind and muscle and heart they invest every day to help maintain and enhance our quality of life.

"Building Michigan" is dedicated to those unsung heroes who have contributed so much to our lives, and to making our great state one of the most beautiful in the country.

— Dale Fisher

Foreword

GOVERNOR JENNIFER GRANHOLM

In Pursuit of Progress

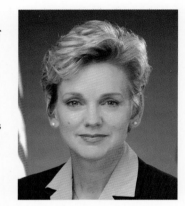

In every way, Michigan has been shaped throughout its history by people of incredible vision and creative energy. Our spirit of innovation and our ethic of hard work created not only the industries that are mainstays of our state, but the structures that stand tall across our peninsulas.

As you travel throughout Michigan – as you gaze at our cityscapes and historic buildings or trek the crisscross of our roads and bridges – you quickly recognize the incredible debt we owe to those generations that came before us. It's a debt to men and women whose sheer determination built our state and created so many of the technological and engineering advancements that we depend on to this day. The people who built Michigan laid the foundation for a new generation of workers whose skills use that technology to reach new heights every day.

Truly, our structures and roadways were born of some of the most talented visionaries. They saw something in their minds the rest could not see until their vision became a reality of steel and stone, built with strong hands and great minds. Engineering feats like the Mackinac Bridge, for example, would have been impossible to conceive of only a few decades before it was actually built. Yet, thanks to the human talent, materials, and equipment that converged to span the Straits of Mackinac, today the Mighty Mack stands as an inspirational reminder of the vision that continues to drive Michigan into the 21st century.

Building Michigan is a beautiful tribute to Michigan's construction industry. While no volume could truly reflect all that has been accomplished, the pages of this book paint a portrait of the people and industry that have contributed so much to our way of life and so much to our state. As you turn the pages, it will be hard not to imagine future contributions, inspirations, and the generations that will be shaped by them in decades to come.

    —Jennifer M. Granholm
     Governor

Foreword

STATE REPRESENTATIVE GENE DEROSSETT

Michigan's Transportation Industry

This morning, I drove to work along the city streets of Lansing with ease and confidence. Later today, I will attend a meeting that requires me to use one of our efficient, well-designed state highways to get me there safely and on time. This evening, I will drive home along a rolling country road that brings me to the familiar and peaceful street where I live.

I don't have to worry about whether the roads to my destination will be there, or what condition they will be in. They are no longer the wooden planks and rutted country lanes we relied on in the early 1900's and before. Michigan's roadways are truly marvels of modern engineering and construction, and they facilitate the travel of literally hundreds of thousands of people every day.

The dedicated individuals working in the road building profession have truly helped Michigan "get out of the mud" by building nearly 10,000 miles of state trunk line highways, 7,000 additional miles of country roads, and over 100,000 miles of country roads and city streets that crisscross the state. These vital assets allow us to conduct our business and our lives without hindrance from our transportation network.

In addition, every citizen of this state is impacted by Michigan's commitment to rebuild, repair, and maintain our road and bridge infrastructure. Our transportation system remains one of the cornerstones of our state's economic success, and we can ill afford to allow our roadways to be anything less than efficient and reliable. Especially with Michigan's global trade network, we must consistently meet high standards of transportation dependability in order to continue to thrive.

We hold the entire road building industry in very high regard, and congratulate the many talented individuals who have contributed to the development of our transportation network. I sincerely appreciate your efforts and extend the best wishes of my colleagues in the Michigan Legislature for your continued success and safety in all future endeavors.

We're counting on you.

Representative Gene DeRossett

Message

MICHIGAN DEPARTMENT OF TRANSPORTATION

Dear Mr. Fisher:

Congratulations on the publishing of your book, "Building Michigan." Your book details eloquently the remarkable story of the building of Michigan's highway system. It is a tribute to the men and women who built our magnificent transportation system, and it fills a previously unaddressed gap in the history of our great state.

As Director of the Michigan Department of Transportation, I take great pride in the achievements of the men and women of MDOT, and in the private road construction and materials industry, for the tremendous job they have done in building Michigan's transportation system into one of the finest in the nation, and world. Michigan motorists drive on nearly 120,000 of improved road surface and 11,000 bridges maintained year around by state and local road crews. Just a few decades ago a trip from our southern border to the furthermost point of the Upper Peninsula took days — now it can be done in just a few hours.

Building roads in Michigan was an innovative process. Our unique topography, soil conditions and multiple freeze/thaw cycles make road construction a challenging process. Thanks to the ingenuity, persistence and just plain hard work of our road and bridge construction professionals, our state's outstanding transportation infrastructure was built efficiently, safely and quickly. From 1960 to 1970, over 1,000 miles of trunkline was built (an average of one mile every three to four days). As is true today and throughout our history, Michigan set the standards in road construction — drawing national attention with the first mile of concrete road (1909, Woodward Avenue in Detroit), first "super highway" (1920s – Davison Highway, Detroit), invention of the center line, first use of aerial surveys, first roadside picnic tables, the first border-to-border interstate (I-94, Detroit to New Buffalo) and others.

This book, "Building Michigan," is a wonderful testament to the men and women who were in the forefront of these achievements. It is a long-overdue historic look at the transportation leaders and workers in our state — and their courage, persistence and dedication in making our system what it is today. On behalf of our state transportation employees, and our partners in the road building and materials industries, thank you.

Gloria J. Jeffs

Acknowledgements

"Building Michigan" was not an easy project to bring to life. The production of this book, starting with an idea written down on a piece of napkin in 1998, to final printing and distribution in late 2003, required hundreds of hours of flying with four different pilots, months of pouring over photographs to find just the right images, and a tremendous effort to communicate the vision of the project to those we hoped would benefit the most: members of the construction industry. We are extremely grateful to the labor unions and corporate sponsors that backed the project financially, and provided the foundational support that was needed to make this book a reality.

There are also many people who contributed their time, talents and energy to "Building Michigan." First and foremost, Patti Lyons, who provided her relentless persistence, untiring effort, and continuous support during months of long and tedious hours searching and organizing our archives of thousands of photographs. She fielded hundreds of phone calls and inquiries about the project, managed several large direct mail campaigns to corporations and organizations throughout the State of Michigan, attended meetings and helped with numerous presentations to labor and contractor organizations. Perhaps most notable of all, she didn't actually lay a hand on me and kept me more sane than I've admitted to her.

Among the many others that truly made a difference in the success of the project, certainly Sam Hart stands out as a tremendous supporter of "Building Michigan." In very simple terms, this book would not have been possible without his frequent and genuine encouragement, and his unwavering willingness to spread the word to those he believed would benefit by participating in this tribute to the construction industry. My sincere thanks and appreciation also go to John Hamilton, who stepped up to follow Sam as the new leader of Operating Engineers Local 324, and acted as a liaison by setting up meetings with the executives of other construction labor unions to promote the book. To Tony Milo from MRBA for recognizing the value of this project from the very beginning, and giving of his valuable time to help make the book a reality. To John Malloure, a tireless promoter of the book, and the most active member of our Advisory Board, who went above and beyond the call of duty to support our efforts and secure sponsor commitments. To Kevin Koehler, the new President of the Construction Association of Michigan (CAM), for sending out over 4,500 letters about the book and publishing a wonderful article about the project in the CAM Magazine. To David Miller, Associate Editor of CAM Magazine, who provided editorial support and helped with caption development. And a special thanks to Jimmy Cooper and Ron Kolsalka, executives of Laborer's Local 1191, who have provided their steadfast support over the entire five years it took us to get the book from first concept to print.

To Charles Edwards, otherwise known as "Professor Pixel", for his invaluable work with digital imaging during many late nights and long weekends, and who taught me ten times what I thought I knew about the digital process. To Christi Clark, the CEO of Martopia, who spent every Saturday morning with us for many months to provide her marketing expertise and organizational support. To Tom Putters of Echo Publications for his patience, expertise and knowledge in graphic design, who pulled this entire project together with style. And finally to Bill Fry, our printer, who has given us ideas, printed samples, and acted as more of a partner than a vendor throughout the entire production of "Building Michigan."

—Dale Fisher

Advisory Panel

Although I have published four other books, "Building Michigan" is the first time I have relied upon the ongoing feedback and input of an advisory board. We were very fortunate to have had the valuable advice and participation of those who agreed to sit on this advisory board, attend meetings, talk to their colleagues and associates about the book, and gather information that helped us make the final photograph selections.

I sincerely appreciated the help and support this group of professionals freely provided, and wish to acknowledge them here, as follows:

Deborah K. Angstrom
Office Coordinator
Operating Engineers Local 324,
Journeyman & Apprentice Training Fund, Inc.

Richard O. Brunvand
Director of Marketing and Public Relations
Michigan Chapter AGC

Ellin M. Callahan
John Carlo Incorporated

Bart Carrigan
Executive Vice President
Michigan Chapter Associated General
Contractors of America, Inc.

Christie Clark
Chief Executive Officer
Martopia

Jimmy Cooper
Business Manager
Laborers' Local 1191

Patrick Devlin
Detroit Building Trades Council

Gary L. Ganton
Training Director,
Operating Engineers Local 324, Journeyman
& Apprentice Training Fund, Inc.

John M. Hamilton
Business Manager
International Union Operating Engineers,
Local 324

Sam T. Hart
Business Manager (1988-2003)
International Union Operating Engineers,
Local 324

Kevin N. Koehler
President
Construction Association of Michigan

Ron Kosalka
Treasurer
Laborers' Local 1191

Patti Lyons
General Manager
Dale Fisher Galleries

John E. Malloure
C.A. Hull Co., Inc.

David R. Miller, C.I.T.
Associate Editor
Construction Association of Michigan

Anthony C. Milo
Executive Vice President
Michigan Road Builders Association

Michael A. Nystrom
Assistant Executive Director
AUC, Michigan's Heavy Construction
Association

Gregory A. Sudderth
President
Construction Industry Resources, Inc.

The Pilots

The control motions of a helicopter are far more subtle than those of fixed wing aircraft. To fly a helicopter requires a set of highly technical and sophisticated skills. It also is a very demanding art. Add to the mix a photographer trying to capture images with just the right light, angle and perspective, and the required piloting skills become nearly impossible to find. Not only must the pilot control the helicopter, he must also have a feel for composition, a unique sense of timing, and an understanding of what the photographer is trying to accomplish. These are the four pilots whose outstanding skills made the images contained in this book possible:

Brian McMahon, owner of McMahon Helicopter Services, is, in Dale's estimation, the finest photographic helicopter pilot in the world. Working together for more than 25 years, Brian and Dale have mastered the intense concentration, coordination and other skills required for creating photographic art from a helicopter.

Nicholas McMahon, a talented young man who learned the fine art of helicopter flying from his Dad, Brian. He could find no better teacher, and has tremendous natural ability. I look forward to watching his progress as he continues to polish his skills and perfect the delicate "touch" required for this type of flying.

Vern Johnson has been flying longer than I have, and that's really saying something. When I think of a pro, someone who can perform flawlessly each and every time, Vern is the man who comes to mind. Not only is he a superb pilot, he is also an accomplished helicopter mechanic, and spends winters in Florida building small helicopters from the ground up.

Siguard (Siggy) Tfeifer is the new kid on the block in that I just started flying with him this year. I was truly amazed at how quickly he understood what I needed him to do, and I enjoyed his personal style and exceptional ability as a pilot.

Brian McMahon

Nick McMahon

Vern Johnson

Siggy Tfeifer

U.S. 131 Bridge over St. Joseph River
Contractor: C.A. Hull Company

"Give 'Em a Break" Campaign
The "Give 'Em A Break" campaign is coordinated by a coalition of interest groups concerned about construction zone safety in the state. Primary sponsors of this annual public information campaign include the Michigan Department of Transportation, the Michigan Road Builders Association, AUC, Michigan Laborers, Operating Engineers Local 324, and others. The coalition sponsors an annual statewide press conference and invests nearly $250,000 per year television, radio and billboard advertisements across the state. The primary message of the coalition is to urge motorists to slow down in highway construction zones.

Road builders in the early 1900s.

Road builders
in 2003

An early 1900s shovel brigade.

Old U.S. 12 in 1918 in Grass Lake, Michigan. Photo courtesy of Leroy Darwin.

U.S. 127 north of Lansing

Carrie Harding at the Sam T. Hart Education Center, Howell

The National Association of Women in Construction (NAWIC) is an international organization with over 6,500 members. Its core task is to enhance the success of women in the construction industry. There are four NAWIC chapters in Michigan located in Lansing, Grand Rapids, Detroit, and Battle Creek-Kalamazoo. NAWIC chapters promote professional education through monthly meetings and construction careers through the NAWICK K-12 programs. All four NAWIC chapters in Michigan offer scholarships to young men and women who are college-bound. The Lansing NAWIC chapter also offers the Tradeswomen Apprenticeship Grant for apprentices who are registered in a bona fide program approved by the USDOL Bureau of Apprenticeship and Training.

University of Michigan Mitchell Field Parking lot
Metropolitan Asphalt Paving Incorporated

Waterland Construction
rebuilding ramps on U.S. 23

M-14 near Ann Arbor
Constructing permanent median barriers

M-14 over Main Street, Ann Arbor
Bridge replacement by C.A. Hull Company

Thornapple River Bridges near Grand Rapids
C.A. Hull was the prime contractor, steel supplied by PDM Bridge

Interchange at US-131 and M-6

(Above) The $141 million interchange at US-131 and M-6 in the Greater Grand Rapids area is the largest single highway project that the Michigan Department of Transportation has carried out to date (as of this writing in Fall 2003). Impressively, the interchange was built while maintaining northbound and southbound traffic through the jobsite with minimal disruption to the flow of traffic. The C.A. Hull Company performed construction of all of the project's bridges, retaining walls and sound walls. The work included 27 new bridges, 18 retaining walls, and 296,000 square feet of sound wall. Major items included 54 miles of foundation piling, 2.5 million cubic feet of poured concrete, 1.86 million pounds of steel bridge girders and 5.9 miles of pre-cast concrete bridge beams. This three-way joint venture also included Kamminga & Roodvoets, Inc. (K&R) of Grand Rapids, Michigan, who performed all earth excavation and embankment plus all underground utility installation and relocation. Ajax Paving Industries, Inc. was responsible for all concrete paving work. Various stages of construction are shown on the following five pages.

(Opposite page) Looking South along US-131, the four new bridges are built awaiting the paving on the new M-6 roadway. The new structures, while not open to the public help contractors move across the project form East to West with interfering with the continuous flow of traffic on us-131. At ground level, US-131 is being completely reconstructed one side at a time while maintaining traffic for the convenience of Grand Rapids drivers. Northbound traffic is flowing at the far left roadway that is to become the "collector-distributor" road for exiting and merging traffic. Southbound traffic is flowing temporarily on the new pavement, second roadway from the left, installed previously for the permanent location of US-131 North.

US-131
(Right) Both North and Southbound traffic is being maintained on the existing on the permanent Northbound mainline and "collector-distributor" (C-D) roadway while crews work on the new Southbound UDS-131 and related C-D roadway.

US-131
(Above) Earth excavation is seen progressing on Northbound US-131while North and Southbound traffic share what is normally the Southbound Roadway. The excavation work consists of removing the original road's slope to make room for another lane to be used by vehicles exiting onto the new M-6 freeway. The slope will be replaced by a new retaining wall at the edge of MDOT's property, which will hold sand fill in place making room for the new lane.

M-6 Bridges
(Left) The four bridges shown will carry M-6 East and Westbound "mainline" on the two bridges in the middle with the related C-D roadways on the two outer bridges. The far right bridge was completed earlier than the schedule required to provide access from East to West for heavy equipment and construction vehicles. The other three bridges will have their gaps filled when the traffic flow is minimal on weeknights. The bridge beams will be erected at night with protective wooden decking temporarily placed to separate normal traffic flow from construction activities above.

US-131 & M-6 Interchange
A high view of the new US-131 / M-6 interchange gives a perspective of the scope of the State's largest highway project. Looking from West to East along M-6 five bridges can be seen carrying M-6 over Clyde Park. Further East (toward top of page) the interchange with US-131 can be seen with the related circular or "cloverleaf" ramps. Further East M-6 crosses the Buck Creek, an active rail line and Division St. on its way to meet with I-96 at its Eastern end.

Sound wall panels are being erected on one of several sound walls on the interchange to insulate residents from the sight and sound of the new M-6 and the expanded US-131 freeways. The sound wall consists of a concrete "H-beam" securely anchored in the ground with concrete panels slipped into the slot of the H-beam post stacked to the required height. The entire network consisted of 900 concrete posts and 296,000 square feet (6.8 acres) of concrete panels.

US-131 and M-6
Looking South near the 68th Street bridge workers are using the 150 ton capacity crane to complete a new retaining wall make room for the "collector-distributor" (C-D) roadways in the foreground. When completed, two roadways will pass under the single span bridge under construction. These roads will bring Westbound M-6 to (left) and Eastbound M-6 (right) drivers onto Southbound US-131. Drivers exiting Southbound US-131 will be driving on top of the new bridge on their way to 68th Street. The 68th St bridge was completely rebuilt to 5 lanes the pervious year.

I-475 & I-69 near Flint
C.A. Hull rehabilitated bridge decks that they had originally constructed in 1973.

U.S. 131 S-Curve project
The U.S. 131 S-Curve project consisted of a mile long S-curve series of bridges capable of carrying 120,000 vehicles per day over the Grand River and into the city of Grand Rapids. PDM Bridge participated in the project as the structural steel fabricator, shipping 262 truckloads of steel in the course of only two months. The northbound structure consists of 243 curved plate girders and 16 wide flange girders. The southbound structure consists of 206 curved plate girders and 20 straight girders. This structure required over 340,000 bolts to complete the assembly. The expedited delivery allowed the project to be opened to traffic one year ahead of schedule. The finished project is shown on the following page.

The Mackinac Bridge
The official history of the Mackinac Bridge began on July 1, 1888, when Cornelius Vanderbilt, at the first meeting of the board of directors of Mackinac Island's Grand Hotel, stated: "We need a bridge across the Straits." Legislation was enacted in 1950 to create a bridge authority to look into the feasibility of a bridge that could span the five-mile distance. The Authority consulted with three of the world's experts in long-span bridge engineering and sought advice on physical and financial feasibility. The bridge project officially began on May 7 and 8, 1954, at St. Ignace and Mackinac City. The project employed as many as 3,500 workers at the bridge site. Designed by Dr. David B. Steinman, the bridge was the longest suspension bridge in the world when completed (a title held until 1998), with a main span length of 3,800 feet and towers that rise 552 feet. The bridge was opened to traffic, on schedule, on November 1, 1957.

**Blue Water Bridge
(also shown on previous page)**
The second Blue Water Bridge is 1,480
feet (451 meters) long and joins Port
Huron, Michigan, to Sarnia, Ontario over
the St. Clair River. PDM Bridge fabricated
the U.S. half of this three-span
continuous steel tied arch bridge jointly
with a Canadian firm, Canron, utilizing
CNC (Computerized Numerically
Controlled) drilling equipment. It required
over 1,600 shop drawings. The American
and Canadian firms built each half of the
bridge in close collaboration, but
independently from one another, while
joining forces in the middle to connect
the two — a wonderful symbol of the
international cooperation between the
U.S. and Canada. The Blue Water Bridge
was named Prize Bridge winner in the
Long Span category for the year 2000.

Proud laborers on the Blue Water Bridge, Laborers' Local 1191

The Ambassador Bridge

The Ambassador Bridge linking Detroit and Windsor, Ontario, opened for traffic on November 15, 1929, nine months ahead of schedule despite engineering firm McClintic-Marshal's last-minute decision to change the already installed but possibly defective cables in the summer of 1929. Close to two miles of cable within cable within cable—37 strands, each as big around as a strong man's biceps and composed of 218 individual sinews of cold drawn, galvanized steel—support the bridge. With a 1,850 foot center span and a total length of 7,490 feet, the bridge was the longest suspension bridge in the world at the time. The U.S. and Canadian terminals are 1 3/4 miles apart. The roadway is 47 feet wide with an eight-foot-wide sidewalk on the west side. The twin silicon steel towers, built on concrete piers resting on bedrock 115 feet below the surface, rise 386 feet above the ground.

The Ambassador Bridge Plaza
facing Canada, I-75 on the right.

New bridges over I-75, Ambassador Bridge in the background

I-75 bridges south of Detroit

I-496 near Lansing
The $45 million project on I-496 near Lansing, Michigan, consisted of eight miles of concrete freeway reconstruction, five total bridge replacements and 27 bridge rehabilitations, all of which were completed in 163 days as a three-way joint venture between the AnLaan Corporation, Midwest Bridge Company, and J. Slagter & Son Construction. Completed bridge shown on next page.

I-496 near Lansing
Completed bridge on I-496.
For construction information, see previous page.

The International Bridge
The International Bridge spans the St. Mary's River and carries international traffic between Sault Ste. Marie, Michigan and Sault Ste. Marie, Ontario. It is the only vehicular crossing between Ontario and Michigan within a 300-mile distance. The International Bridge is located at the northern terminus of Interstate I-75 and forms a critical gateway linking Canada and the United States. The bridge also plays a vital role in the well-being of both Soo communities. It serves as an essential transportation link to the steel, paper and forest industries, to tourism-reliant business, and to the general public for work, recreation, and shopping purposes. In 2001, 2.49 million vehicles crossed the bridge.

8 Mile Road at Telegraph
New 8 Mile bridges over U.S. 24 (Telegraph Road), in Southfield constructed by E.C. Korneffel.

Milk River Bridge, St. Clair Shores
Early construction of the decorative Jefferson Avenue bridges over the Milk River in St. Clair Shores.

Completed Milk River Bridge, St. Clair Shores
E.C. Korneffel constructed decorative Jefferson Avenue
bridges over the Milk River in St. Clair Shores.

U.S. 23 Huron River Bridge
These bridges, rehabilitated by Slagter Construction, are located on US 23 over the Huron River in Washtenaw County. The job consisted of a bridge deck overlay, new barrier railings, full-depth deck with repairs, and sub-structure repairs and scour protection of the river bottom, along with guard-rail safety improvements.

The Life Sciences Institute and Bio-Medical Science Research Building on the campus of The University of Michigan
John E. Green is responsible for all plumbing, HVAC, and process piping in the University of Michigan's Life Sciences Institute.
This facility, one of a complex of buildings known as the Palmer Drive Development, is due to be completed in the late Fall of
2003. The 235,000 gross sq. ft. building consists of six floors and a mechanical penthouse. It will accommodate the newly created
Life Sciences Institute, whose purpose is to enhance the education, basic research and translational research in the life sciences at
the University. Approximately 150,000 net square feet of space will house "wet" research laboratory and laboratory support spaces,
core laboratory areas, principal investigator offices, interaction spaces, the Institute's administration offices, a combined
gallery/lobby space and a small library. Along with the research building, the Institute staff will have the ability to use
complementary facilities at other buildings on the site including: computational laboratories, "dry" labs, conference and meeting
facilities, a 140-seat lecture space, and food service facilities.

The Bio-Medical Science Research Building on the campus of The University of Michigan is a $180 million project for Spence
Brothers. The firm is completing all concrete and general trades work for the 472,000 sq. ft. facility, comprised of five above-grade
floors and two below-grade floors. Construction on the immense structure is due to be completed in December 2005.
(also see next page)

The Life Sciences Institute and Bio-Medical Science Research Building on the campus of The University of Michigan (also see previous page)

Central Park residential development, Shelby Township
Central Park is a new residential development located in Shelby Township on Van Dyke between 22 & 23 Mile Road. The site was originally owned by the Packard Motor Car Company as their proving grounds, and was purchased by Curtis Wright. Ford Motor Company later purchased it in the 1950s. Of the original 600 acres, Ford adopted a master plan that called for 100 acres of single family, 75 acres of multi-family, 79 acres of industrial, 31 acres of parkland, 14 acres of Packard preservation, 6 acres of office and 23 acres of commercial retail. In 2002, Ford rezoned the 175 acres and sold the property to a developer.

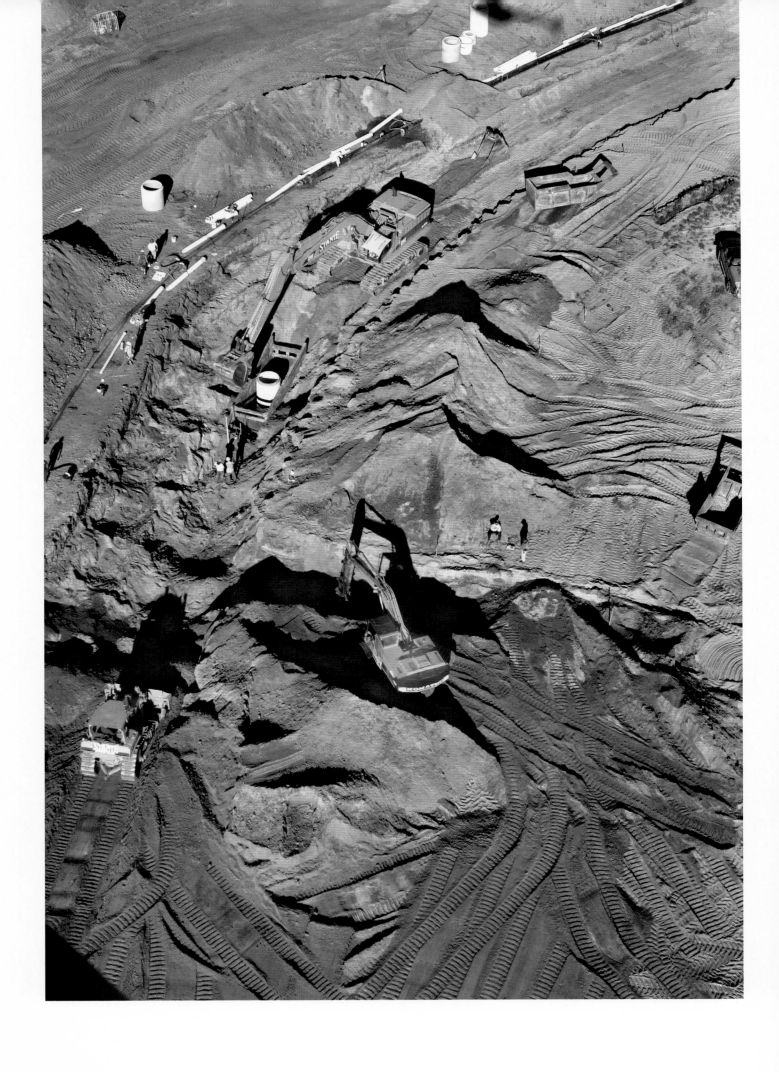

Central Park residential development, Shelby Township
Stante Excavating of Northville is the general contractor of the site work, which includes land balancing, storm sewer, sanitary sewer, water and street paving work. Over 100,000 feet of pipe had to be laid in a four-week time period. In order to meet the September 2003 deadline, on July 19, 22 Mile Road had to be closed to traffic in order to lay sewer pipe in 11 places across the road. Eighteen excavators, 12 loaders and 90 workers were mobilized to accomplish that task in only one day. The project includes 15,000 tons of asphalt paving for six miles of streets in the development.

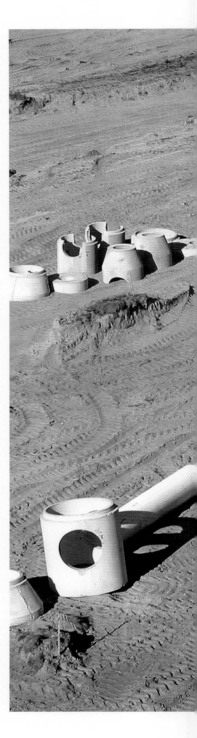

Stante Excavating's Michigan CAT equipment hard at work.

Central Park residential development, Shelby Township
Stante Excavating

Central Park residential development, Shelby Township

Central Park residential development, Shelby Township

General Motors Grand River Assembly – Lansing
Beginning phase of construction of General Motors' Lansing Grand River Assembly Plant. When completed, the plant could employ 1,320 hourly and 180 salaried workers at full two-shift capacity.

American Axel & Manufacturing – World Headquarters – Detroit, MI
The headquarters of American Axel and Manufacturing will be situated on a
19-acre parcel at I-75 and Holbrook Avenue in Detroit, a site that is already
part of the company's 174-acre campus. Five hundred employees will be
housed initially in the new facility with an influx of an additional 200 people
transferring from other locations. The exterior construction features glass
curtain wall and architectural pre-cast panels, giving the building a striking
façade. The ground floor will house a full-service cafeteria and an auditorium
with seating for 300 people, and a parking deck for 650 spaces.

Consumers Energy – Jackson

Consumers Energy's new headquarters in downtown Jackson – its corporate home for 117 years – incorporates a U.S. Post Office constructed in 1932 and designed by a Jackson native, Claire Allen. The new headquarters creates office space for 1,200 employees of Consumers Energy and its parent company, CMS Energy, and will result in reduced facilities costs for the company. Constructed on a former brownfield site, the project was a joint effort by the Company, the City of Jackson, the Michigan Economic Development Corporation, the U.S. Environmental Protection Agency and other organizations. John E. Green Company was the mechanical contractor. An extensive public space and RiverWalk trail along the Grand River are part of the community benefits of the new headquarters setting. Consumers Energy, the principal subsidiary of CMS Energy, provides natural gas and electricity to more than six million of the state's nearly 10 million residents in all 68 Lower Peninsula counties.

St. Joseph Mercy Hospital – Ann Arbor

John E. Green was the prime mechanical contractor for the 554-bed St. Joseph Mercy Hospital built at the Catherine McAuley Health Center. John E. Green has completed numerous projects and major remodeling, including renovation of the 10,000 square foot third floor OB unit creating new maternity suites complete with in-room whirlpool baths. They were also the mechanical contractor for the 240,000 square foot Reichert Professional Medical Building at the same site.

Historic St. Joseph Mercy Hospital before multiple additions

Helipad at University of Michigan Hospital

The University of Michigan Health System's helipad is situated on a sliver of land that slopes almost 50 feet down to the edge of a retention pond. The structure is supported by 11,000 face feet of segmental retaining wall and is linked directly to the emergency room by a tunnel that was bored underneath the hospital roadway.

North Tunnel, Detroit Metropolitan Wayne County Airport Midfield Terminal
The North Tunnel Project at Detroit Metropolitan Wayne County Airport is one of the brightest jewels in the New Midfield Terminal Project Crown. This six-lane tunnel project required temporary closure of the airport's major crosswinds runway and several busy taxiways. This element made for a challenging project. The location of the project site, in the highly restricted AOA of the airport, required exact timing of material delivery and strict adherence to a very complex schedule. One of the earliest successes of the project was the record setting concrete slab pour where Walbridge Aldinger poured 21,000 cubic yards of concrete within one 24-hour period. The nearly complete tunnel project will be one of the first new pieces of the Midfield Terminal Project that visitors see when driving to the new terminal. Walbridge Aldinger was involved in many other portions of the Northwest Airlines Detroit Metropolitan Wayne County Airport Midfield Terminal project.

Detroit Metropolitan Wayne County Airport Midfield Terminal
The Edward H. McNamara Terminal / Northwest WorldGateway
serves Northwest Airlines and their partner airlines —
Continental, Mesaba and KLM, as well as Lufthansa. The 2
million-square-foot, state-of-the-art facility is shown in various
stages of construction on the following pages.

Detroit Metropolitan Wayne County Airport Midfield Terminal

Detroit Metropolitan Wayne County Airport Midfield Terminal

Detroit Metropolitan Wayne County Airport Midfield Terminal

Detroit Metropolitan Wayne County Airport Midfield Terminal in operation.

Ford Field
Few visitors will realize the technical expertise that was required to transform a downtown Detroit location into a quality sports venue. Ford Field's domed roof is supported by a 10,500-ton structural steel truss system. The entire system was constructed on the ground and lifted in two stages. Precise engineering was required to design and erect the 8.23-acre curved roof.

"When asked to help construct a new stadium that would lead to the return of the Detroit Lions to the downtown area, we couldn't have been more thrilled to participate. Handling the Owner Controlled Insurance Programs for the construction of Ford Field is exactly the kind of risk related business programs Marsh has been providing customers in Michigan for the past 80 years. This one was a real pleasure!"
—Gregory Stanbury, Partnership Head, Midwest Region / Marsh

Warren Army Tank Plant
Tanks no longer roll from 24-hour assembly lines at the Warren Army Tank Plant as they did during the height of World War II, but the site along Mound and Interstate 696 in Warren, Michigan, is still in the business of keeping the nation secure. Engineers at the U.S. Army Tank-automotive and Armaments Command (TACOM) do their work these days on computers. TACOM's research and development operation is the city's third-largest employer with 3,500 people, mostly white-collar employees, working within the walls of the facility.

Visteon Village

In early 2002, Walbridge Aldinger was named Construction Manager for Visteon Corporation's major corporate consolidation project in Van Buren Township, Michigan—Visteon Village. The site is centrally located in the heart of Southeast Michigan and will accommodate roughly 4,000 employees from 14 current office locations. The 265-acre parcel incorporates a 35-acre man-made lake, surrounding woodlands, lies within 5 miles of two major airports (including Detroit Metro International Airport) and is adjacent to major freeway access. Construction includes nine separate buildings totaling an approximate one million sq. ft. of office, manufacturing and technical space. The main structure, called Town Center, includes several unique areas of development. It houses customer presentation and training areas, product displays, central IT functions and an upscale cafeteria. The campus also includes boardwalks and a nature trail for public and employee use.

Comerica Park
Turner Construction provided pre-construction and construction management services for the $250 million Comerica Park project. The 40,000-seat ballpark, new home of the Detroit Tigers, features no outfield seats in its upper bowl and along the ballpark's south side; a wrought iron fence is all that stands between the sidewalk and fans outside the park. This unique design allows people on the outside to see what's happening on the inside of the ballpark while giving fans inside the park an unobstructed view of downtown Detroit. Completed in 2000, the project included a 1,000 car parking structure, 1,500-space parking lot and related infrastructure improvements.

Compuware Headquarters
Another Walbridge Aldinger construction site is the Compuware Headquarters Phase I building, which is a 16-story facility oriented along Woodward and Monroe Avenues, with a strong physical orientation toward the Campus Martius Park in downtown Detroit. The street level of the building has street-oriented retail and restaurant spaces along the entire frontage. The facility includes a fourteen-story atrium, corporate offices, a cafeteria, a training center, a wellness center, a day care facility and other supporting spaces for approximately 3,000 employees. Parking is provided for all 3,000 employees in a two level underground parking structure directly beneath the building and extending under Farmer Street to the Crowley Block and in a connected nine-story above grade structure above the Crowley Block. Exterior materials of the building feature classical and durable materials, including stone, metals and high-performance clear glass.

Delphi
The Delphi Automotive Systems Headquarters in Troy consists of a 160,000 square-foot, six-story office tower and a 100,000 square-foot technical center. The ultramodern complex reflects the high-tech nature of Delphi's operations, as well as the superior skill of Michigan contractors.

Ford Rouge Plant

Ford's Rouge Complex in Detroit is one of the oldest operating factories in the world. The new Ford Rouge Center will embrace Ford's heritage of innovation and business strength through design for a sustainable, dynamic, and prosperous future. The Ford Rouge Center will implement economically and ecologically intelligent workplace and manufacturing operations, while preserving 3,000 jobs at the complex. The first phase of the project includes a new 600,000 square foot assembly plant.

This new building features skylights for day lighting the factory floor, mezzanine-level worker services and circulation, and the largest planted "living roof" anywhere in the world. The assembly building's green roof, combined with other landscaping strategies, provide natural storm water management, potentially saving Ford millions of dollars. Walbridge Aldinger, along with architects William McDonough & Partners, will build a new body shop and innovative assembly plant as part of a $2-billion renovation and expansion of the historic Rouge industrial complex. Other improvements include: proposed supplier park, UAW Family Learning Center, High-tech training facility, and a possible visitors center and tour program.

The Basilica of St. Mary Antiochian Orthodox Church
The Basilica of St. Mary Antiochian Orthodox Church is a replica of the 4th century basilica built in North Syria. The architectural design expresses its beauty and its theology, worship and mission. The church was designed by Angelos Demetrious and is located at 18100 Merriman Road in Livonia, Michigan.

The Basilica of St. Mary Antiochian Orthodox Church during construction

The newly-renovated Blessed Sacrament Cathedral, Detroit

Jefferson Wastewater Treatment Plant
The new PC-740 Clarifier Project at the Jefferson Wastewater Treatment Plant for the Detroit Water & Sewerage Department is Walbridge Aldinger's latest in 20 continuous years of construction with the department. Walbridge Aldinger serves as the construction manager for the project, which includes new construction of two 300 ft. diameter clarifiers, and renovation of four existing clarifiers. The project is scheduled for completion in the Fall of 2003.

Jefferson Wastewater Treatment Plant clarifiers

Jefferson Wastewater Treatment Plant

Ypsilanti Community Utilities Authority (YCUA) Wastewater Treatment Plant
A 2 1/2 year project to expand the existing Ypsilanti Community Utilities
Authority (YCUA) Wastewater Treatment Plant to over 1 1/2 times the existing
capacity calls for plant updating, more odor controls, safer disinfection
equipment, expansion of screening, grit removal, primary settling, aeration, final
settling, tertiary filtration, effluent pumping, related site improvements and a
more efficient incinerator for burning sewage sludge to replace the current unit.
A major part of the project for the John E. Green Company is installation of
biosolids thickening and dewatering, biosolids cake handling, conveying,
pumping and loading facilities. Engineers estimate air pollution will be reduced
by more than 80% when the project, which includes the replacement of the
existing multiple hearth biosolids incinerator with a modern, fluidized bed
incinerator, is completed.

Connor Creek CSO Control Facility
Connor Creek CSO Control Facility is located at Maheras-Gentry Park off Clairpointe Street along the Detroit River, and is a Detroit Water and Sewerage Department and the Detroit River Heritage Navigator project. Connor Creek is a combined Sewer Overflow (CSO) Control Facility for watershed groups, DWSD wholesale customers and basin neighbors. The $187 million project is the largest of Detroit's four CSO basins and recently received the Environmental Management Association's Outstanding Achievement Award. In addition to controlling Michigan's largest CSO outfall, the project includes dredging Connor Creek and rehabilitating a Detroit River coastal habitat.

Coal Fired Power Plant – Monroe
Four massive Selective Catalytic Reduction (SCR) units are being constructed to reduce NOx (nitrogen oxides) emissions at the Monroe Power Plant. A Manitowoc 21000 series crane with a lift capacity of 1,000 tons has allowed the project team to adopt a modular installation approach, doing much of the work at ground level and then lifting large components into place. An 18-inch thick reinforced concrete pad was poured specifically to accommodate the huge machine. At the time this book was published, two of the four SCR units were completed.

Chrysler Technology Center, Auburn Hills, Michigan
Walbridge Aldinger is a contractor for the Chrysler Technology Center (CTC) in Auburn Hills, Michigan. This 3.5 million sq. ft. office, R&D, computer, light manufacturing, training and data center has been designed as the center of all automotive research and development for Daimler Chrysler. It brings more than 7,000 of the company's engineers, designers, and technicians into one central location. CTC is comprised of 28,000 tons of steel, 260,000 square feet of glass, 400,000 square feet of metal panels, 170,000 cubic yards of concrete, and 1.5 million square feet of roofing. This mega-structure spreads out over 138 acres and rises four stories at its highest point. It consists of approximately 16 separate areas under one roof.

Lansing's State Capitol

The State Capitol is Michigan's most important historic building. It has received national recognition for its extraordinary architecture and art. The building was dedicated on January 1, 1879. After more than one hundred years of weathering, neglect, hard use, and structural and technological alterations, the Michigan Legislature in 1987 established the Michigan Capitol Committee and charged that body with overseeing the building's restoration and maintenance.

It was not the goal of this committee to create a museum, but to retain it as the modern working seat of Michigan state government: the place where, for at least the next one hundred years, the Legislature and the Governor can continue to address the issues that confront the citizens of our great state. The restoration period took three years, from 1989 through 1992. The building was rededicated on November 19, 1992.

Saginaw Valley State University

Saginaw Valley State University
Spence Brothers managed and constructed the Regional Education Center at Saginaw Valley State University. This $30 million facility is the home of the highly respected and growing College of Education, as well as the Alan W. Ott Auditorium with state of the art audio/visual technology. It also houses the Regional Educators Resource Center, providing resources and teacher instructional facilities for educators throughout mid-Michigan. Construction was completed in August 2003.

Coast Guard Station on the St. Clair River
E.C. Korneffel Company

Phipps-Emmet Office Building (above)
High-tech office users that need the best in data transfer and communication access will occupy the Phipps-Emmet Office Building in Plymouth, Michigan. It will be a lease building with 20,000 square feet on three floors and was 90% completed when this image was taken. It is a steel structure with brick veneer, and one of three buildings in this planned development on Beck Road.

The New Liberty Bank (left)
The New Liberty Bank on Ann Arbor Road in Plymouth, Michigan, is shown here in the foundation stage. The three-floor, 20,000 sq. ft. structure will serve as the bank's corporate headquarters. Designed in a federalist style with brick veneer exterior, the steel structure also will be used for walk-in banking traffic with teller lines as well as commercial lending and private banking. Emmet Construction Company.

Grass Lake High School
A brand new high school for the growing community of Grass Lake consisted of a $2.6 million dollar mechanical/plumbing project. This state of the art facility utilizes a heat pump reverse return system with 3 energy recovery units to heat and cool the building. This system allows for maximum energy efficiency during both the heating and cooling seasons. The building also houses the best in educational resources such as science and laboratory rooms, a media center and computer laboratories, each requiring specialty cooling equipment supplied and installed by John E. Green Company.

Ford High School for the Fine, Performing and Communication Arts – Detroit, MI
Joint venture partners L.S. Brinker Company and Skanska USA Building, Inc. are construction managers for this high school in the heart of Detroit's cultural district. The seven-story, 296,649 square-foot building is being built next door to the Detroit Symphony Orchestra. The facility layout is developed around a plan for a six-story building plus one mechanical story occupying all of a two-acre site with off-site parking. The high school portion of the facility will include classrooms, labs, offices, art rooms, computer graphics lab, cafeteria and kitchen for 1,200 students in grades 9-12. The building will also incorporate spaces open to the public including one main auditorium with numerous rehearsal and practice halls as well as support rooms where students can take full advantage of contact with professional musicians and other working artists. The building will also house the new production center for Detroit Public Television WTVS (Channel 56), the local PBS affiliate, and a new radio facility for WDTR, the Detroit Public Schools FM radio. When the Fine, Performing and Communication Arts High School is complete, the 285,000-square-foot structure will feature an operating radio station, 800-seat performing arts auditorium, recital hall and television studios. The building's location behind Orchestra Hall will ensure that exposure to the arts will expand beyond its walls.

New Cass Technical High School
Cass Technical High School has a 90-year reputation for education excellence. Being constructed next to old Cass Technical High School, this spectacular facility will continue the legacy for years to come.

Joint training venture between the Operating Engineers 324 and
Iron Workers Local 25 at Sam T. Hart Education Center, Howell.

Doubletree Hotel and Conference Center, Bay City, Michigan
A Turner Construction project underway is the $24.3 million Doubletree Hotel and Conference Center in Bay City, Michigan. The hotel and conference center will reside on the east bank of the Saginaw River, enabling a spectacular view of the city. The first class facilities will include a 150-room Doubletree Hotel and attached 24,000 square foot Conference Center with a total of 310 parking places. Completion is slated for February 2004.

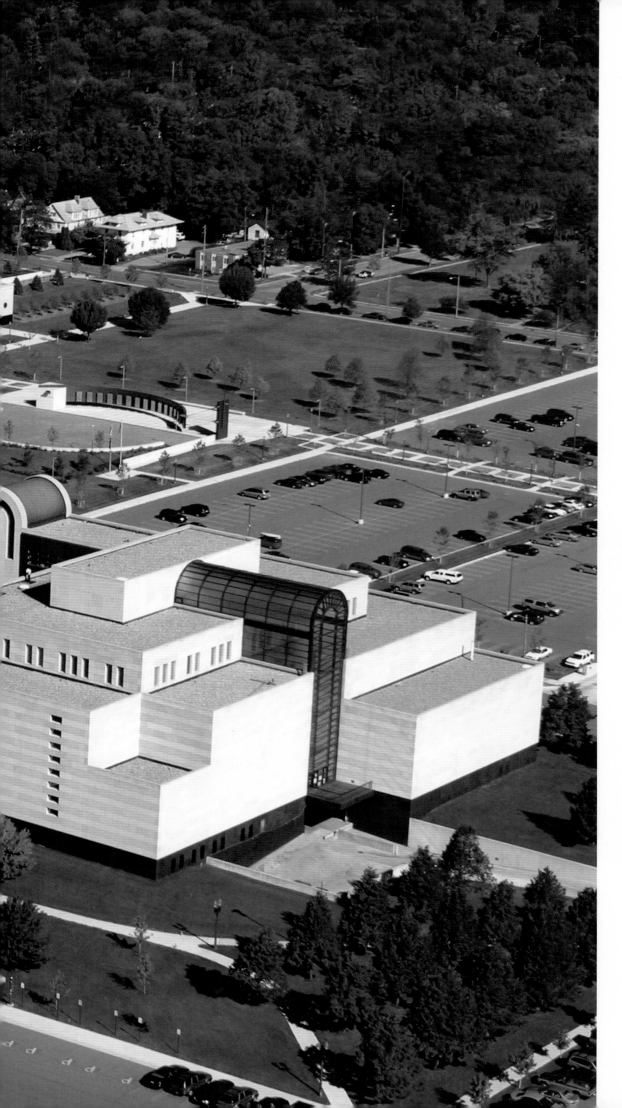

The Michigan Vietnam Memorial, Lansing

The Michigan Vietnam Memorial is a massive arc of steel bearing the names of the 2,649 Michigan service people who were killed or are missing in action. The memorial is an eight-foot tall, 117-foot long steel archway, surrounded by an illuminated walkway. The arch holds the individual name plats on the monument site, and is located at All Veterans Park in Lansing, between the Hall of Justice and the Michigan Historical Museum.

Major supporters of the $2.6 million project included the United Auto Workers Region 1 and the Michigan Nursery & Landscape Association in donations of trees and landscape materials. Donations from veteran's organizations across the state and from individuals were instrumental in raising $1.7 million to get the project underway.

Michigan Hall of Justice

The Michigan Hall of Justice consolidates the Supreme Court, Court of Appeals, and State Court Administrative Office into a new 281,000-foot facility with underground parking for 460 cars. The curved shape and character of the building reflects the complex architectural and engineering design, which provided cost effective and innovative solutions. The Hall, which provides the state's judiciary's first permanent home in Michigan's history, was completed in October 2002.

The Solanus Casey Center

The International Masonry Institute and Bricklayers and Allied Craftworkers Union (BAC) Local 1 Michigan had a significant part in the construction of the $13 million Solanus Casey Center. The 44,000-square-foot pilgrimage complex, next to St. Bonaventure on Mt. Elliott, north of Lafayette, features gardens for reflection and meditation, museum space on the history of the Capuchin Friars and the life of Father Solanus, common areas, a 90-seat auditorium, 120-guest dining area and kitchen, spiritual counseling center, and houses the tomb of Father Solanus. The two-story facility is accented with brick and stone details, Pewabic tile, a glass gable roof, gallery and bookstore. The center was a significant upgrade from the current center and is designed to accommodate bus tour groups. Visitor counts are expected to increase from 60,000 to over 100,000 per year with the opening of the new facility and upon declaration of sainthood for Father Solanus.

The John D. Dingell VA Medical Center

The John D. Dingell VA Medical Center, located in downtown Detroit, became fully operational in June 1996. This state-of-the-art facility replaced the Allen Park VA Medical Center built in 1937. The Dingell VAMC provides primary, secondary and tertiary care including acute medical, surgical, psychiatric, neurological, dermatological, and intermediate inpatient care. In addition, both primary and specialized outpatient services are provided at the medical center as well as outpatient substance abuse, day treatment, and a mental hygiene clinic. The VAMC operates 134 hospital beds and 84 nursing home care beds. The medical center supports two off-site primary care clinics in Yale, Michigan, and the old Allen Park VAMC site and two communities based Veterans Outreach Centers in Detroit and Lincoln Park, Michigan.

The John D. Dingell VA Medical Center is affiliated with the Wayne State University School of Medicine and serves as a training site for medical students and for graduate medical training to medical residents and fellows. Other medical care disciplines trained in the medical center include nurses, social workers, and psychologists. The VAMC also has an active medical research program with research funding of approximately $3 million.

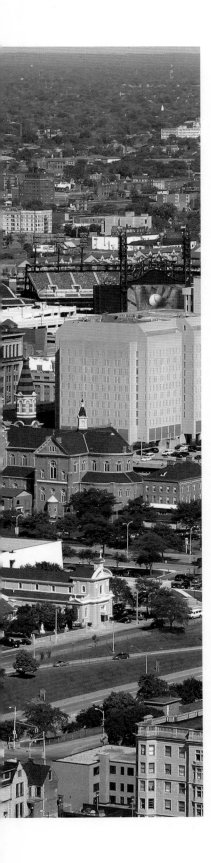

Blue Cross & Blue Shield
The brilliant blue and white signage of
Blue Cross & Blue Shield is being lifted
by McMahon Helicopter to its new
destination within the rich tapestry of the
Detroit skyline. Fast-paced construction
transforms the Motor City into an ever-
changing monument to the quality of
Michigan construction.

Arctic Ring of Life, Detroit Zoo
Turner Construction's Michigan office provided pre-construction and construction management services for a 2.4-acre polar bear exhibit and 12,000 sq. ft. amphibian center at the Detroit Zoo. The Arctic Ring of Life exhibit takes visitors on a virtual trek to the North Pole. Guests to the Zoo experience the tundra, open sea and pack ice of the Arctic environment, and the animals that are distinctively adapted to life there.

The Detroit Institute of Arts
The Detroit Institute of Arts is undergoing a massive renovation and expansion project that includes a four-story, 35,000-square-foot addition to the south wing, increased gallery space and extensive infrastructure upgrades.

African-American Museum
The African-American Museum features a 100-foot diameter dome making it a visual centerpiece of the Detroit Cultural Center. Bricklayers Local 1 Michigan and International Masonry Institute

Photo by Claude Jodoin

Anchor Bay High School
Bricklayers Local 1 Michigan and International Masonry Institute

Grosse Pointe Yacht Club, Grosse Pointe Shores, Michigan

The unique swimming pools built by Camps Services and Aristeo Construction for the Grosse Pointe Yacht Club in Grosse Pointe Shores, Michigan, are situated on a peninsula on the waterfront, only a few feet away from the yachts owned by many of the club's members. The 5,216 sq. ft. competition-size pool has eight racing lanes and a one-meter high diving board. The 936 sq. ft. training pool is split into two parts divided by a waterfall. The more shallow area of the training pool has a mushroom water feature in which children love to play. Both swimming pools have stainless steel gutter systems to keep the water level stable.

Southgate Community Recreation Center, Southgate, Michigan

The two beautiful and elaborate swimming pools of the Southgate Community Recreation Center, Southgate, Michigan, were completed by Camps Services and Aristeo Construction under tight scheduling constraints determined by the needs of the owner. The 5,917 sq. ft. indoor pool consists of five areas: the lesson area, the splash area with water features and toys, the lap area, the spa area and the plunge area, where the slide exits into the pool. The 9,977 sq. ft. outdoor pool also consists of five areas: the aerobics/fitness area, the lap area, the spa area, the splash area with water features and toys, and the plunge area where the slides exit into the pool. Both pools have zero depth entry and a stainless steel perimeter overflow system to keep the water level stable. The outdoor pool also features a 166-foot long flume slide/body slide and a spa area that has a separate warming area and hot tub.

Waterford Oaks Park, Waterford, Michigan
Construction on the 12,250 sq. ft. wave pool at Waterford Oaks Park in Waterford, Michigan, began in the spring and needed to be finished in time for a Memorial Day opening to the public. In a matter of weeks, Camps Services and Aristeo Construction installed a new mechanical system, including all new wave-making equipment. New water features and toys were also added to give the patrons of the park more enjoyment. A variety of manufactured palm trees and rocks were installed to give the park a tropical look.

GM Tech Center

The General Motors Tech Center is located on more than 850 acres in Warren, Michigan. GM has spent nearly $1 billion on renovations and additions to the 47-year-old Tech Center in recent years. Additions include a 12-acre outdoor theater, an eight-story tower and a man-made lake. The tower, called the Vehicle Engineering Center, provides a workplace for 8,000 engineers. The Tech Center houses GM's largest concentration of employees, more than 23,000, and is the largest site for automotive engineering in the world.

Vector Pipeline
The Vector Pipeline is a 348-mile, 42-inch pipeline project in the U.S. and Canada that transports natural gas from the Chicago area to parts of Indiana and Michigan into Ontario, Canada. Construction took place during 2000 and Vector began operations December 1, 2000. The Vector Pipeline is owned by a joint venture including Enbridge Inc., Duke Energy Corporation, and DTE Energy Company of Detroit, Michigan.

Moving a pipeline due to Detroit Metro Airport Expansion.

Newaygo Waste Water Treatment Plant
Davis Construction's Concrete Division (Grand Rapids) is the
general contractor on the Newaygo Waste Water Treatment Plant,
currently under construction.

Newaygo Waste Water Treatment Plant

**The Henry Ford
Greenfield Village**

As a part of The Henry Ford Campus in Dearborn, Michigan, Greenfield Village is a National Historic Landmark. Built in 1929 by Henry Ford, Greenfield Village is the nation's largest outdoor museum and welcomes 1.5 million visitors annually. In September 2002, Walbridge Aldinger (WA) and Greenfield Village began construction of the Underground Restoration Project. WA coordinated the design and construction efforts in order to create a new utility infrastructure for the Village. The new utilities include electricity, natural gas, water and storm/sewer, security wiring and communications. Instead of 17 streetlights, 330 lights now line the Village paths in order to make nighttime functions possible. Walbridge Aldinger relocated 12 of the historic buildings, renovated two buildings (The Village Store and Gatehouse) and constructed two new buildings (The Crafts and Trades Buildings and Catering Pavilion). Throughout construction, Walbridge value engineered $1.85 million and accommodated 34 design revisions.

Greenfield Village Renovation Behind the Scenes
The 81-acre, $20 million Greenfield Village Infrastructure Restoration Project began in 2000 with an initial engineering study, which AUC – Michigan's Heavy Construction Association – helped coordinate and fund. An invitation to become involved in the project was extended to AUC members by Greenfield Village. Following a series of meetings between Greenfield Village and AUC members, the initial estimate of $29 million was reduced by $10 million because of the efforts of AUC association members who donated time, effort, equipment, materials and value engineering, which uses the most innovative methods, practices and materials available to complete the restoration at the reduced costs.

A significant amount of financial support was added by other trade unions that included: Michigan Laborers & Employers Cooperation and Education Trust, Local 1191, Local 324 LECET, and Operating Engineers Local 324 Labor-Management Education Committee.

All AUC member companies and 500 employees involved in the project will have their names permanently etched in stone at the Village entrance in recognition of their services. There has never been a collaboration effort like this one before, where competitors–who usually go head to head with one another – came together under such extremely difficult conditions to take on different facets of a project.

AUC members replaced almost all of the existing sanitary sewers, water mains, storm sewers, irrigation piping and natural gas piping. All electric and communications were upgraded and expanded in new underground duct banks and conduits. Parking was created and roads within the Village were completely reconstructed with new concrete and asphalt as well as new sidewalks.

In addition, a new millpond was created and a bridge erected at the new crafts and trades area. All told, three miles of gas, sewer and water lines were replaced, 5,000 miles of electrical and fiber optic line were installed, along with replacement of seven miles of roads and three miles of sidewalks. Of the 22 companies that completed all work by June 2003, each company worked on a time and material basis with no profit or home office overhead charged.

The Henry Ford
Greenfield Village

Fredrick Meijer Gardens, near Grand Rapids

Early morning, Detroit

Grand Rapids cityscape

Detroit – looking south

Laborer's Legacy Monument

Members of the Laborers, Operating Engineers, Cement Masons, and other Detroit-area unions cleared the land in front of Hart Plaza, installed steel rods, set the foundation for the circular base, and built the two walls of honor.

The Landmark's 63-foot-high stainless steel arch rises above the base. Some of the companies that built the memorial were Turner Construction, Aristeo, and Walbridge Aldinger. The Greater Detroit Building and Construction Trades Council and the Associated General Contractors of America, Greater Detroit Chapter, have provided help for the project.

The landmark's arch is open at the top to symbolize labor's unfinished tasks. An arcing light connects the arch's two sides and symbolizes the labor movement's energy. At the base are 14 bronze reliefs, each mounted on a six-foot-high granite boulder, which describes labor history in Detroit and projects labor's hope for a better world.

The Soo Locks
The Soo Locks are a vital and key point in the Great Lakes navigation system, which affects eight states within the United States, Canada, and ultimately the world's mariner commerce traffic. Ships that pass through the Soo Locks have come as far away as Russia to pick up goods and resources from ports like Duluth. The U.S. Army Corps of Engineers, Detroit District, has operated and maintained the entire facility at the St. Mary's Canal in Sault Ste. Marie, Michigan since 1881. This engineering marvel consists of two canals and four locks: Davis Lock, Poe Lock, MacArthur Lock, and the Sabin Lock. Each lock allows vessels of many types and sizes to safely traverse the 21-foot drop in elevation of the St. Mary's River between Lake Superior and Lakes Michigan and Huron. More than 11,000 vessels carry more than 90 million tons of cargo through the locks each year. The Corps has plans to replace the Davis and Sabin Locks with a larger, state-of-the-art lock, similar to the Poe Lock, to assist in handling the larger vessels of the Great Lakes fleet. The new lock will be the first lock built at the Soo since 1968.

Petoskey, Michigan
Namesake of Michigan's state stone, Petoskey is tucked away in the Northwest corner of Michigan's Lower Peninsula, where Lake Michigan's Little Traverse Bay provides a water playground for residents and its many visitors.

Traverse City Waterfront
Northern Michigan is known for pristine natural beauty, but construction contractors
that have provided modern amenities for visitors to enjoy are equally responsible for
Traverse City's emergence as a tourist destination.

Grand Traverse Resort and Spa
The Grand Traverse Resort and Spa is situated on 900 acres in northwest Michigan's Lower Peninsula, six miles northeast of Traverse City. The resort opened in 1980 as a 245-room hotel and conference center and by 1986 the 17-story glass enclosed Tower was completed featuring 186 spacious rooms and suites. Today, 660 guest rooms, 85,000 square-feet of versatile meeting space, a full-service spa, and 54 holes of championship golf featuring courses by Jack Nicklaus, Gary Player, and William Newcomb make the resort the Midwest's largest full-service, year-round destination resort and conference center.

Frankenmuth, Michigan
Octoberfest draws thousands of
visitors to this replica of a
Bavarian town each year.

Pfizer's Technical Development Facility, Ann Arbor

Turner Construction was part of the construction of Pfizer's Technical Development Facility in Ann Arbor, Michigan, which was a $185 million project completed in 2002. This 435,000 square foot facility includes research and development, product development, and a laboratory-office complex of two major buildings: the laboratory and office building, and the development building. The buildings bring all technical development functions closer to other R&D related functions. In addition to the buildings, the project includes a tunnel that passes below Huron Parkway to connect to the dining and meeting facilities elsewhere on the Pfizer campus.

Michigan International Speedway
Michigan International Speedway boasts a proud 35-year history of hosting
America's best racing action on its 1,200-plus acres in the scenic Irish Hills.
With 18 degree banking and 73-foot wide sweeping turns, Michigan
International Speedway provides drivers with three and four grooves to run
around the two-mile speedway. Since its opening in 1968, the success of the
speedway and the growth of motor sports have made Michigan International
Speedway the largest sports arena in Michigan. The center grandstand seats
over 27,000. In 1999, a 28,000-seat, 10-1/2-story high structure was added
to the center grandstand, increasing the number of seats to 55,000.

Wayne State University's Williams Mall Undergraduate Residence Hall
The $20 million Wayne State University Williams Mall Undergraduate Housing project provides an environment properly suited for more conventional animals —370 college students. Turner Construction provided the design-build services for the 128,000 sq. ft., six-story block and plank frame structure clad in WSU's standard brick color. The residence hall includes a 380-seat dining hall, ground floor offices, conference rooms, retail, and student apartments. The building is adjacent to the undergraduate library and is across from the Student Center and the Recreation and Fitness Center.

Central Michigan University campus expansion

University of Michigan stadium

Eastern Michigan University stadium

Michigan State University Spartan stadium

Michigan State University Pavilion for Agriculture and Livestock Education

Troy cityscape

VA Medical Center – Ann Arbor
In foreground of above photo, the recently completed 340,000-square-foot clinical addition seen here is a state-of-the-art medical facility that was designed to meet the complex medical needs of military veterans. The University of Michigan Medical Center can be seen in the background.

(left) University of Michigan North Campus

Bay Harbor Golf Club
The Bay Harbor Golf Club is one of the most picturesque golf sites in the country. Beautifully poised upon the stately bluffs overlooking Lake Michigan and Little Traverse Bay.

Indian Community Center, near beautiful Suttons Bay

(opposite page) The Round Island Lighthouse
A familiar sight to visitors of Mackinac Island for more than a hundred years, the Round Island Lighthouse was placed into service on May 15, 1896. It marked the channel between Round Island and Mackinac Island, the shortest distance from northern Lake Huron to the Straits of Mackinac. Three keepers were stationed at the lighthouse, but their families lived at nearby Mackinac Island. In 1947, the Round Island Lighthouse was abandoned, replaced by a functional but unattractive light closer to Mackinac Island. The U.S. Forest Service took possession in 1958, and it is now part of Hiawatha National Forest. Severely damaged by storms and high water over the years, the old lighthouse has been receiving much needed clean-up and structural help since the 1980s by many organizations including the Friends of the Round Island Lighthouse, the Hiawatha National Forest, the Mackinac Island Historical, Boy Scout Troop 323 and the Great Lakes Lighthouse Keepers Association.

Fort Mackinac

Although Fort Mackinac had been well maintained, Band-Aid solutions that were designed to keep the fort in operation only delayed the need for a complete overhaul. As work began on the largest reconstruction project in Fort Mackinac's history, the rough limestone walls were so unstable that the longstanding tradition of firing the cannon from the South Wall every hour on the hour was temporarily suspended. Contractors then removed stones in a controlled break, which caused water-damaged portions of the wall to collapse without bringing down the entire wall.

Limestone, quarried on Mackinac Island, was the original stone building material for the fort. As time progressed, water formed small cavities in the stones. Contractors checked each stone with a hammer to determine which stones had hidden water inside that could undermine their strength. Over 90 percent of the fort's original stones were salvaged and combined with 250 tons of dolomite limestone that should be more resistant to water damage.

The project team developed subtle improvements, some of which actually restored elements of the fort that were identified from historic photographs. With the project complete, Fort Mackinac is in better condition than it was when it was built 220 years ago.

AnLaan Corporation

AnLaan Corporation was incorporated in 1986 by current president and treasurer Don Anderson and current Vice President and Secretary Gerrit Ter Laan. The firm, which is located in Ferrysburg, Michigan, carries out both public and private construction projects involving bridge-related items of work such as sheet piling, foundation piling, and structural concrete.

In 2003, the firm added key field staff in the important area of bridge rehabilitation. In addition to many bridge removal and replacement projects in Michigan counties and municipalities as well as private bridge projects, the firm was the lead partner, along with Midwest Bridge and Slagter Construction, for the $46 million project to fix I-496, the main transportation artery in and around Lansing, Michigan and part of the overall "Capital Loop"

project.

This young but growing firm received the 1997 Michigan Quality Initiative Achievement Award for its work on the I-94 Business Loop/M-43 Road and Bridge Construction Project. In 1998, the American Society of Civil Engineers presented the firm with their Quality of Life Award for their live repair to Muskegon County's 66" diameter force main.

Associated Underground Contractors (AUC)

AUC Michigan's Heavy Construction Association represents the interests of over 550 members statewide. When AUC (Associated Underground Contractors) was founded 55 years ago, the majority of its members were underground contractors. Since then, the organization has expanded to include many other areas in Michigan's heavy construction industry such as road/bridge building, electrical contracting, painting, plus more, and thus became AUC Michigan's Heavy Construction Association.

Member companies receive a variety of services, including labor relations, legislative representation, construction safety services, regulatory involvement (Michigan Occupational Safety and Health Administration, Michigan Department of Transportation, Michigan Department of Environmental Quality, etc.), utility damage consultation, seminars, and publications.

In recent years, AUC has worked extremely hard for the successful passage of Proposal 2, which authorizes the state to issue $1 billion in bonds to correct problems with the state's sewer and storm water systems. The problems of aging underground infrastructure impact the Great Lakes, rivers and streams, which are polluted regularly by sewage overflows. Other successful legislative initiatives over the years have proved AUC's commitment to fight for meaningful issues that affect above ground and underground construction companies throughout Michigan.

Blue Cross Blue Shield

of Michigan

Salutes Michigan's Construction Industry

Blue Cross and Blue Shield of Michigan has come a long way since its humble beginnings 64 years ago. The company started with three employees and one telephone on the 10th floor of the Washington Boulevard Building in Detroit.

Since then, the company has grown to provide health insurance benefits to 4.8 million Michigan residents.

To accommodate the growing business and to solidify its commitment to the community, Blue Cross broke ground in 1971 for the Detroit Service Center – the company's landmark headquarters on Lafayette in Detroit. This building stands 22 stories and includes a recessed courtyard, which houses the largest freestanding bronze sculpture in North America.

Over the next two decades, the Blues completed construction of nearly a dozen office and parking facilities around the state. The design and functionality of these structures showcase the skill and expertise of Michigan's construction industry.

Blue Cross Blue Shield Blue Care Network of Michigan

C.A. Hull Company

On September first of 1999, the C.A. Hull Company of Walled Lake, Michigan, passed what the company considers a milestone in its history; it was on the same date in 1954 that the company was first incorporated. C.A. Hull's beginnings date back to the era of Michigan road building when earth excavation was performed with horse drawn implements. During this period, Clarence Hull and his father were active in the dirt business. Clarence worked for his father doing the related concrete work found on earth moving projects, which consisted of building headwalls and culverts. Clarence's concrete work evolved into a proprietorship in his name in the late 1940s.

In the 1950s, Clarence hired a young engineer by the name of Don Malloure. Malloure had attended the University of Michigan, receiving a degree in civil engineering on the G.I. Bill after serving in the U.S. Navy. Malloure approached Clarence about an employment arrangement that included an ownership provision. They agreed to form a new business called C.A. Hull Co., Inc. in 1954 with Don Malloure as a minority shareholder. The agreement was to be that Malloure would acquire the balance of the company over ten years, but the new business was to proceed only if an upcoming letting by the Michigan State Highway Department (MSHD) was successful. If it was not, Clarence Hull planned to sell the business and retire. Needless to say, a bid to build a bridge that would carry what is now I-75 over a rail spur in Monroe County was a success and C.A. Hull has continued to grow and thrive. By 1965, Malloure had acquired 100% ownership of the company, and in 1966 when Clarence Hull passed away, the future of the company was left to him.

Today's C.A. Hull is bigger than it was

M-5 and I-96

during that era; it has grown to one of the largest bridge-building firms in Michigan. It has advanced technologically with the changing times, too, but the foundation that was laid so many decades ago is still intact and C.A. Hull is a tough competitor in the MDOT letting arena. Don Malloure is still interested and involved in overseeing the company, but now many of the operational duties are administered by the next generation of Malloure engineers; his sons Joe, John and Paul all play integral roles in managing the company and its projects. Joe Malloure is now

president of the company, and John and Paul are both Vice Presidents. According to Joe Malloure, over 90% of the company's work comes from being the low bidder on MDOT contracts. They do a large portion of their work in Michigan's lower peninsula concentrated in the Detroit metro area, but have done jobs in the U.P. and out-state areas. Although Hull is primarily a bridge contractor, they also do some concrete paving, marine work and excavating.

Grosse Pointe Yacht Club, Grosse Pointe Shores, Michigan

Aristeo Construction

Aristeo Construction has earned an excellent reputation for 26 years by meeting the needs and expectations of our clients. Founded in 1977, we have evolved from being an excavating and concrete contractor into a full-service contractor/construction manager with a full array of self-perform and general contracting capabilities. We are poised to act as a single source for all project needs — equipment, maintenance, manpower, and management.

With sales volume in excess of $80M, our success has been earned every day, on every project. We earn it by continually improving our operating processes, which emphasize quality and client satisfaction. In January of 2000, Aristeo became ISO 9001 certified. During 2002, the Company committed itself to making the transition to ISO 9001:2000 standards and to pursuing ISO 14001:1996 certification. We successfully completed both pursuits and are proud to earn these stamps of approval. They ensure our clients

benefit from a comprehensive set of quality and environmental standards accepted throughout the country.

Our 63,000 FT_ facility in the metropolitan Detroit area includes our steel fabrication shop, equipment maintenance shop, warehouse, and administrative offices. We consistently respond to clients' needs throughout the United States with projects in Michigan, Indiana, Ohio, Kentucky, Illinois, Missouri, Minnesota, Wisconsin, Virginia, Arizona, Florida, and New York. We will continually expand our geographic responsiveness to meet our clients' needs. Aristeo remains poised to deliver quality solutions based on 26 years of experience, an excellent safety record, financial stability, equipment fleet with a replacement value in excess of $15 million, and a dedicated workforce nearly 300 strong. Simply stated, we listen to our clients and employ the resources to get the job done.

Camps Services

In 1957, Samuel Camp, aged 22, began work as a laborer for a Michigan-based pool company. With the experience he learned there, plus additional positions within the construction industry, he and his family founded Camps Services, Ltd., in 1983. Twenty years later, Camps has grown into one of Michigan's leading commercial pool construction and service companies.

Our customer base consists of apartment complexes, county clubs, condo associations, swim clubs, motels, hotels, community pools, and school systems. To each project we bring the full force of our most important asset – our hard-earned reputation, a reputation firmly established by striving for excellence with each project we undertake. Our team brings to each assignment a strong work ethic, a determination to succeed, and, most importantly, a sense of humor.

Construction Association of Michigan (CAM)

Previously known as the Builders Exchange of Detroit and Michigan, the Construction Association of Michigan (CAM) was founded in 1885, and is the oldest and largest regional construction association in North America. CAM is a not-for-profit association of design and construction professionals. Its 4,000+ membership includes contractors, architects, engineers, suppliers and manufacturers.

Accurate and timely information is essential to gain the competitive edge! Services that allow a business to operate at peak efficiency are vital! The Construction Association of Michigan provides its members with solid information and premier services.

CAM is the leading source and authority for construction news and research in Michigan. Its members rely on these CAM publications to stay ahead in this competitive, challenging industry: _Construction Project News_, a daily report providing complete details on bidding activity throughout the state; _Construction Pre-View_, a weekly publication filled with detailed information about projects still in the design stage; the award-winning monthly _CAM Magazine_ with fascinating feature articles on Michigan's construction industry; and the annual _Construction Buyers Guide_, long recognized as the most comprehensive directory of

construction service providers in Michigan.

CAM members keep pace with the constantly changing world of technology with _Electronic Construction Project News_ and the _Electronic Construction Buyers Guide_, both available at www.cam-online.com.

Member benefits include Construction Federal Credit Union, a federally chartered full service credit union; the CAM Benefit Program, providing group health insurance; and

CAM Workers' Compensation, a self-insured compensation program. CAM's Labor Relations Service provides participating union contractors with a reliable source of information and assistance in their interaction with organized labor.

CAM's Training and Education Center (CAMTEC) offers specialized classes and timely seminars on subjects and issues that directly affect the

construction industry. Construction professionals attending CAMTEC can receive training on modern construction management methods, Michigan construction laws and new safety regulations.

CAM co-sponsors _Design and Construction Expo_, held annually since 1985, the largest construction exposition in the Midwest. More than 15,000 owners, developers and buyers of construction services attend annually.

The Construction Association of Michigan promotes and supports the construction industry, and provides leadership through ongoing legislative relations, professional development and public awareness initiatives.

East Paris Bridge over new highway M-6 in Grand Rapids.

Davis Construction Inc.

Davis Construction, Inc., of Lansing and Grand Rapids, Michigan, was founded in 1968 and began as a residential home contractor, with just a handful of employees. Within just ten years, the firm has expanded into the commercial and industrial markets, specializing in concrete and earthwork.

The most recent addition was in 1992, when Davis Construction began building many Michigan bridges. Davis Construction is proud to maintain four divisions with more than 100 employees: concrete/commercial building, earth-work and bridges. The firm is MDOT Pre-qualified, a member of the MRBA, and a member of AUC.

MAJOR RECENT PROJECTS CARRIED OUT BY THE FIRM INCLUDE:

• Aldi Distribution Warehouse, completed by Davis Construction's Dirt Division. Davis's portion of the project was all earthwork, foundation excavation, roads and parking areas, storm and sanitary pipe. Bovis Lend Lease was the General contractor on the project. The total project was completed in July 2003.

• The Bridge Division of Davis constructed the entirely new East Paris Bridge over M-6.

• The Bridge Division also removed and completely replaced the Charlotte Highway Bridge over the Grand River.

• Davis Construction's Concrete Division (Grand Rapids) is the General Contractor on new plant Newaygo Waste Water Treatment Plant currently under construction.

E.C. Korneffel Co.

E.C. Korneffel Co. in Trenton, Michigan, provides heavy civil services from the design to implementation phases for all types of piling work, deep water port facilities, earth retention systems and bridge construction. Our expert staff is prepared to meet the most stringent demands and toughest challenges in the construction industry today. Since our formal incorporation in 1950, E.C. Korneffel Co. has earned the distinction as the premier foundation piling and earth retention contractor in the Detroit Metropolitan area.

Notable projects include over 7,000 bearing piles for the new Ford Motor Heritage Project in Dearborn, Michigan; 4,500 piles for the new Northwest Detroit Metropolitan Airport expansion project and the last two Deep Water Port Facilities constructed in Detroit, as well as the only two of its type, King Pile installation projects for deep intake structures for the power generation industry. Included are foundation systems for the new Dearborn Industrial Generation Power Plant and for the Kinder Morgan Power Plant in Jackson, Michigan, as well as the new Calpine Energy Center in Fremont, Ohio.

In August of 2003, our foundation system began the process for the new Lafarge Cement relocation effort, paving the way for the re-development with new casinos in the downtown Detroit Riverfront District. Fast track projects are our specialty, having completed the Lafarge work in 18 working days. With our fleet of over 250 pieces of major equipment, including nine above boom point pile driving rigs, we are the contractor of choice when schedule and technical know-how are paramount.

E.C. Korneffel Co. has a second division, that being bridge contractors, performing full service bridge construction for MDOT and other governmental agencies. Our bridge efforts are spent within the State of Michigan and include such structures as the decorative Jefferson Avenue bridges over the Milk River in St. Clair Shores and the new 8 Mile Structures over US-24 – Telegraph Road, in Southfield as well as many others on all of the major freeways in the Detroit Metropolitan Area.

The relocation of the LaFarge Detroit Cement Terminal plays a crucial role in the City of Detroit's continued revitalization effort. As the preeminent deep foundation piling contractor in the Detroit Metropolitan Area, E.C. Korneffel's extensive experience was essential in the fast track installation of 650 HP12x74 bearing piles (rated at a capacity of 150 tons each). Featured in the photograph above are one Manitowoc 3900W and two 2900W crawler cranes. Outfitted with state of the art 110' fixed lead systems and Vulcan 506 (32,500 ft-lbs) pneumatic hammers, the two 2900Ws were instrumental in driving full length 90' members, eliminating the need for costly and time-consuming operations associated with pile splicing. Using a swinging lead system, the 3900W employed an ICE 80S (104,000 ft-lbs) diesel hammer to final drive the piles to capacity. The combination of industry leading specialized equipment and sequentially coordinated division of labor enabled E.C. Korneffel to complete the entire project in a record-breaking 18 days.

Graders and Landscape Association

In the late 1970's, several contractors performing landscape beautification were working on construction projects, and decided there was a growing need to reorganize themselves to become a more viable entity in the construction industry. They met with labor organizations such as Laborer's Local 1191 and Operating Engineer's Local 324, and negotiated a fair and equitable contract for all entities.

The creation of this union, along with their partnership with organized labor has become an intricate part in the finalization of any construction project. Areas within the Graders and Landscape Association's jurisdiction include: Seeding, Sodding, Planting, Cutting, Trimming, Back Filling and Rough Grading.

Although the reins have changed hands from the contractor's negotiating side to the present founders, then including the Reinhold Group, DeAngelis Landscape, and the present W.H.Canon Landscape, throughout the years the association has become a viable and important unit within the construction industry.

Greenfield Village

Greater Detroit Building and Construction Trades Council

Since 1937, the Greater Detroit Building and Construction Trades Council has represented the interests of unionized construction workers in Southeast Michigan.

Our mission is to assure health, safety and fair wage standards for the 35,000 highly skilled construction workers we represent.

The Greater Detroit Building and Construction Trades Council represents the highly skilled construction workers in Southeast Michigan's construction industry.

The council:
- Promotes a fair wage and benefit standard and as well as safe working conditions for the construction workers we represent.
- Coordinates internal activities among our affiliated trade unions.
- Establishes and maintains liaisons with construction contractors, owners and other labor organizations.
- Promotes construction as a career choice.
- Communicates with our affiliated unions and individual members.
- Participates in the collective bargaining process for some workers.

- Takes an active role in the political process with get-out-the-vote efforts, helping the campaigns of candidates who support our goals, and making sure the political process is fair to our members.

Detroit Building Trades Online is dedicated to serving members and local unions affiliated with the Greater Detroit Building Trades Council.

The Building Tradesman newspaper, one of Michigan's oldest labor publications, is featured on-line, dispensing general news of interest to Michigan's construction trades workers.

International Brotherhood of Electrical Workers Local Union #252 and National Electrical Contractors Association (NECA), Ann Arbor Division

Local Union #252, International Brotherhood of Electrical Workers and the Ann Arbor Division, Michigan Chapter, National Electrical Contractors Association are a labor and management alliance dedicated to providing the best in electrical construction and maintenance services.

These two organizations combine the onsite installation skills of the highly qualified electricians from the International Brotherhood of Electrical Workers with the advanced management capabilities of electrical contractors from National Electrical Contractors Association to bring you the highest quality electrical installations in south central Michigan.

The International Brotherhood of Electrical Workers and National Electrical Contractors Association have built the vast majority of the world-class buildings in the Ann Arbor – Jackson area. The Local Union #252, International Brotherhood of Electrical Workers and Ann Arbor Division - National Electrical Contractors Association electrical construction team have developed the most productive partnership in the electrical construction and maintenance industry resulting in top-quality, cost-effective, energy-efficient, industrial, commercial, institutional, telecommunications and residential building projects.

International Masonry Institute

Since the days of one-room schoolhouses, brick has had a reputation for the construction of solid facilities that stand the test of time. Modern-day union masons proudly carry this tradition into the 21st century with the help of The International Masonry Institute (IMI).

IMI operates a National Training Center, as well as 12 satellite centers, that offer training programs at all levels from pre-apprentice to foreman. Training is offered in all the masonry trades; brick, block, tile, terrazzo, marble, mosaic, stone, plaster, pointing/cleaning/caulking and cement. Since this training comes directly from IMI, it far exceeds the quality of training that is usually available at the local level and the curriculum always includes the latest safety and health requirements and techniques.

IMI promotes union masonry through trade shows, exhibits, and craft-specific promotional events, as well as advertising and marketing campaigns. Architects and engineers can also benefit from IMI training programs that are designed to give them hands-on exposure with masonry materials and techniques, helping them to become more familiar with the advantages of masonry. The IMI also offers custom consultations to local and national firms.

Over the years, masonry has evolved into a very complex trade. Through the IMI, union contractors can offer unparalleled quality by keeping abreast of the rapid changes in this fast-paced industry.

Photo by Claude Jodoin

Anchor Bay High School

Bricklayers Local 1 Michigan
International Union of Bricklayers and Allied Craftworkers

The International Union of Bricklayers and Allied Craftworkers is the oldest continuously operating trade union in the United States.

The Bricklayers and Allied Craftworkers Union (BAC) has been serving the members of the trowel trades in the Metro Detroit area since 1897. Detroit BAC Local 1 was chartered in 1994 by merging Locals 2, 26, and 35. Detroit Local 1 represents all facets of the trowel trades industry including Cement Masons, Bricklayers, Plasterers, Stone Masons, Paving Masons, Pointers, Cleaners, Caulkers (Restoration) and Refractory craftworkers.

Local 1 members benefit from above-average base wages, holiday/vacation pay, a local pension, an international pension, annuities, health care, financial services, educational scholarships and student loan programs. Signatory contractors receive a variety of services including labor relations, legislative representation, construction safety services, regulatory participation, contractor education programs, construction guides and other publications and research and development efforts for the masonry industry.

BAC Local 1 Detroit is proud to carry on a tradition of excellence by training and employing the local workforce in constructing and restoring the

The Solanus Casey Center

International Union of Operating Engineers
Local 324

Since its founding in 1906, the Detroit based Local 324 of the International Union of Operating Engineers has been a leader in the union construction movement throughout Michigan. Its present roster of over

construction material suppliers such as sand and gravel producers, concrete and asphalt plants, and in a wide variety of activities that support construction.

IUOE Local 324 members have played essential roles in building such

Habitat for Humanity, and helping Santa Claus in delivering Christmas presents to bedridden children in hospitals.

Charles Paluska (1937-1962), Louis Blok (1962-1966), William Myers (1968-71) Keith Sober (1971-1980), Raymond Poupore (1980-88), Sam T. Hart (1988-2003) have served as business managers, with John Hamilton — who previously served as president — winning the 2003 election for the post. All have guided the local as it developed and improved health care and retirement programs for its members, as well as its Journeyman & Apprentice Training Fund program for the training of apprentices and upgrading of journeyman skills.

14,000 members operate the cranes, excavators, dozers, scrapers, loaders, and related construction equipment that create roads and bridges, drinking water and sewage treatment systems, schools and universities, hospitals and office towers, shopping malls and commercial buildings, electrical power and natural gas facilities, and the whole host of other construction projects that have made modern life possible. You'll find them working for contractors as well as in such shop related functions as construction equipment sales distributors, crane rental companies,

landmarks as Ford Field and Comerica Park, the Renaissance Center, the DaimlerChrysler Technology Center, all of Michigan's automotive and truck plants, the Mackinac Bridge, and the state's interstate and state highway system. During times of crisis members have operated equipment vital for rescue operations, including the tragedy at the World Trade Center, as well as dealt with environmentally threatening spills of hazardous materials. And they've also donated services to communities, helping them build diamonds for Little League Baseball, homes for

IUOE Local 324 was among the first in the nation to establish a Labor-Management Education Committee to work with contractor associations and project owners to enhance the benefits of union construction. The committee is charter member and co-sponsor of the Michigan Fair Contracting Center, which investigates complaints of violations of both state and prevailing wage laws. The center works to ensure workers aren't cheated by non-signatory contractors out of salaries and benefits that are legally specified for public works projects.

John E. Green Company

In 1909, with $20 cash in hand, John E. Green founded a residential plumbing and heating business in Highland Park, Michigan. Throughout the decades, under four generations of management, the company steadily broadened its scope of work and rapidly expanded the business in the industrial and institutional fields, laying the groundwork for what the company is today: one of the largest and most diversified mechanical contractors in the country. Nearly 100 years after its founding, the John E. Green Company's professionals are responsible for the installation of advanced mechanical systems all over the country in every segment of industry.

Several important Michigan projects give an idea of the variety of successful projects carried out by this firm.

- A 2 1/2 year project to expand the existing Ypsilanti Community Utilities Authority (YCUA) Wastewater Treatment Plant to over 1 1/2 times the existing 80%.

- The General Motors World Headquarters at the Renaissance Center project involves the renovation of the commercial multi-use podium, or base, of one of the largest commercial developments in the country.

^a The Life Sciences Institute at the University of Michigan will be a 235,000 gross sq. ft. facility consisting of six floors and a mechanical penthouse

The General Motors World Headquarters at the Renaissance Center project involves the renovation of the commercial multi-use podium, or base, of one of the largest commercial developments in the country. The podium structure contains most of the mechanical and electrical infrastructure for the five high rise towers of the Renaissance Center as well as housing offices, retail, parking, restaurants and other public facilities. This complex project was made more challenging because of unknown conditions, due to the lack of accurate and complete as-built drawings. JEG took the lead in addressing the unknown conditions, both from the engineering and installation processes, with no impact to the completion schedule. The firm, through pre-contract and post-contract Team Design Assist with A/E, CM, and the owner, redesigned the chilled water, heating water and steam distribution systems, revised equipment selection and materials and methods that reduced the mechanical costs by $3.5 million.

Joint training venture between the Operating Engineers 324 and Iron Workers Local 25.

Journeyman & Apprentice Training Fund, Inc.
Sam T. Hart Education Center

Since 1967, the Journeyman & Apprentice Training Fund, Inc. (JATF) of the International Union of Operating Engineers Local 324 has provided continuing education opportunities for Apprentice and Journeyman Operating Engineers at its training and education center in Howell, Michigan. Formerly the Howell Education Center, the facility – now known as the Sam T. Hart Education Center – was named after Local 324's longtime Business Manager who retired in 2003.

Dedicated to providing a new generation of highly skilled construction trade workers for Michigan's construction job market, this state-of-the-art "construction college" is settled on 515 acres and features more than 30,000 square-feet of classroom and shop facilities for technical courses and testing. The education center is the only training facility in

Michigan accredited by the National Commission for the Certification of Crane Operators to provide crane certification testing.

Out back, the site's expansive acreage provides unlimited exercises and hands-on learning opportunities in crane operation, excavating, grading, road building, trenching, disaster recovery, and hazardous materials handling, among other activities. A variety of specialized training programs conducted jointly with organizations such as Ironworkers Local 25 and Michigan Urban Search and Rescue, among others, are hosted at the education center annually.

JATF Apprentices are required to complete a minimum of three years or 6,000 hours of combined classroom and on-site training. Each year the JATF provides thousands of Local 324

members more than 60,000 hours of training and certification courses. Refresher and recertification courses are also offered to help experienced Journeyman Operating Engineers update their skills for changing technologies and equipment advances.

JATF instructors are among the most skilled Operating Engineers in the heavy equipment industry today. Each instructor is an experienced heavy equipment Operator and has received extensive training from the International Union of Operating Engineers, the Occupational Safety & Health Administration, the Michigan Construction Trades Safety Institute, National Commission for the Certification of Crane Operators, and the National Safety Council in addition to numerous colleges and universities where construction applications are taught.

Laborers' Local 1191

Laborers' Local 1191 received its charter from the Laborers' International Union of North America (LIUNA) on September 17, 1937. Today the Local represents more than 3,600 laborers across Michigan. The union has jurisdiction over all highway and road construction work in the state. In addition, Local 1191 members handle numerous other projects including underground, sewer, gas, electric, telephone and landscaping work in Wayne and Macomb Counties.

Working in partnership with the Michigan Road Builders Association, AUC (Associated Underground Contractors) Michigan's Heavy Construction Association, and the Graders and Landscapers Association, Local 1191 created its own Laborers-Employers Cooperation and Education Trust (LECET). This fund is used to promote Local 1191, educate and train members, and generate project and job opportunities.

Laborers' Local 1191 has worked tirelessly to win excellent wages, pensions, health insurance and vacation benefits for its members. The Local actively lobbies for favorable results in issues that affect its members, such as federal and state highway funding, unemployment benefits, construction safety and much more. Laborers' Local 1191 is proud to have maintained a strong and dedicated membership since its inception, including many retirees who have been with the Local for 50 years or more.

Jimmy Cooper, Business Manager
Ronald Kosalka, Secretary/Treasurer

The Blue Water Bridge

Management & Unions Serving Together

MUST is a nonprofit 501-C-5 organization that maintains its budget through joint contributions based on a cent per hour worked from each building tradesmen and is then matched by each signatory contractor association. Here is a listing of the following MUST participants who meet quarterly to discuss matters pertaining to Southeast Michigan's unionized construction industry. Since their founding in 1988, The M.U.S.T. label has meant a total quality construction job.

Since our founding in 1988, the M.U.S.T. label has meant a total quality construction job.

Our Mission

To ensure the highest standards on the MUST label are met through the continuous improvement of safety, quality, and value on construction sites while completing jobs on-time and on-budget with the highest skilled and trained workforce prepared to meet the demands of construction users/developers in Southeast Michigan.

Together building trade unions (representing 30,000 building trades people) and contractor associations (representing 4000 contractors) initiate joint programs designed to optimize performance and meet this mission on all M.U.S.T. construction sites in Southeast Michigan. The extensive network of apprenticeship schools that M.U.S.T. represents, provides the most certifiable, qualified, and job ready candidates for the workforce.

It is the M.U.S.T. label that symbolizes this quality craftsmanship that goes into our construction jobs.

TO SERVE THE USERS OF CONSTRUCTION SERVICES, MUST IS COMMITTED TO:
- Maintaining The Competitive Edge
- Safety
- A Highly Skilled and Trained Workforce
- On Time, On-Budget Performance
- Communication
- Business Attraction
- Community Outreach

Ford High School for the Fine, Performing and Communication Arts – Detroit, MI

Marsh Detroit

When Henry Marsh opened the Detroit office of Marsh in 1914, the business thrived due to the automotive industry and the need to insure the construction of new auto manufacturing plants. That same spirit and commitment continues today, allowing Marsh to help secure the necessary insurance services to complete some of the largest and most creative construction projects ever seen in Michigan. These include Ford Heritage 2000 at the Rouge Complex, Visteon Village, the new Ford Field in downtown Detroit and various projects for Detroit Public Schools.

The concept of insuring risk is not new in today's business climate. Greater innovation in risk and insurance strategies is in high demand. For Marsh Detroit, that means more inventiveness and harder work to continually create new risk management solutions for clients. Clients look to Marsh for innovative programs which will address critical safety issues for construction projects and their workers. They need safe practices, which defines new risks. Marsh Detroit can deliver the structuring, placing and maintenance of risk management solutions that are right for

each firm.

The style and professionalism of Marsh's team creates an approach to problem-solving that sets Marsh Detroit apart from the competition in terms of finding solutions for clients.

As was the vision of Henry Marsh in 1914, Marsh Detroit continues to provide the leadership, the resources and the dedication necessary to meet the needs of southeast Michigan's largest and most influential businesses and their industrial growth challenges and opportunities.

McMahon Helicopter Services, Inc.

McMahon Helicopters is FAA Approved as a Certified Air Carrier for both Air Taxi and Heavy-Lift External Load operations. McMahon uses turbine-powered, Bell Jetranger, Longranger, Bell 222 and large Sikorsky helicopters. McMahon is a Bell Helicopter Customer Service Facility, an FAA Certified Repair Station and the largest helicopter operator in Michigan. McMahon Helicopters is proud to have participated in the building of Michigan for over 22 years.

The Construction Industry utilizes helicopters to survey and photograph building sites. Helicopters are used to lift air-conditioning units, erect signs, set stacks, place antennas, hold steel beams or move heavy cranes to different locations. Helicopters can access areas that would otherwise be completely inaccessible for any other machine. In construction applications helicopters can move men and equipment not just higher, but quicker and easier, allowing contractors to be more efficient and their projects to be more cost effective.

Our lift pilots are used as aerial crane operators; proud members of Operating Engineers Local 324.

McMahon's aircraft are used by the automotive industry for executive transportation and time-critical delivery of parts between their manufacturing facilities. Our helicopters are used by hospitals for emergency-transportation of their organ procurement teams. Our helicopters are also used for television coverage of breaking news, real estate surveys, aerial cinematography, power & pipeline surveys, special security patrols and a variety of other purposes.

McMahon's aircraft have flown congressmen, ex-presidents, top executives and movie stars. Our Helicopters have been used for many feature films and televised sports events, including, coverage of Super Bowl games, Marathons and the Detroit Grand Prix races.

McMahon Helicopters is owned and operated by Brian McMahon and his older son Nicholas. Brian is a Vietnam Veteran, a helicopter pilot with over 20,000 hours and 32 years of experience flying and operating helicopters. Nick is also a pilot and manages the heavy-lift operations.

McMahon has its own custom built aviation facility which is also an FAA Certified Heliport located adjacent to the East side of the Plymouth-Canton Mettetal Airport. www.mcmahonhelicopters.com

Michigan CAT

We began as Michigan Tractor and Machinery Company and are now known as Michigan CAT where hundreds of families are dedicated to improving the livelihood of those who build, move, grow, dig, or light Michigan. This has been our commitment since 1944…to keep you going… day or night.

Though what used to be started with pony motors and run by wire rope is now started by satellites and run by computer, one thing hasn't changed: our desire to improve the quality of life in Michigan and those we work with.

Michigan CAT is the primary source of Parts, Service, Sales and Rentals to most builders of roads, bridges, sewers, water, schools, and developers of commercial and residential sites. We also provide engines and equipment for manufacturing, mining, steel, marine, forestry, demolition, oil natural gas and electricity. Other services include financing, insurance, and software for the construction, manufacturing and maintenance industries.

Michigan Chapter
Associated General Contractors

"Building Your Quality of Life."

The Michigan Chapter Associated General Contractors, Inc. (AGC) is a full service construction trade association serving as the voice of the commercial construction industry in out state Michigan.

- It is one of 101 Associated General Contractors of America Inc. Chapters with 35,000 member firms including 7,500 of the nation's leading general contracting companies.
- There are over 12,000 specialty, and more than 14,000 service/suppliers associated with AGC through its nationwide network of chapters.
- AGC is dedicated to improving the construction industry education, promoting use of the latest technology and advocating building the best quality projects for owners—public and private.

- AGC members are committed to three tenets of industry advancement and opportunity: Skill, Integrity, and Responsibility.

The Michigan Chapter AGC is the only full service construction trade association specifically serving the needs of the general contractor in out state Michigan.

- Established in 1927, the Michigan Chapter AGC provides services for over 200 general contractor and affiliated members, the entire construction industry, a variety of community groups, schools, colleges and universities.
1. Quality insurance programs for members
2. Respective legislative and government relations
3. Labor relations

4. Apprenticeship training and program management
5. Craft worker training
6. School-to-Work training
7. Construction Futures training materials used in fifth grade through high school classrooms
8. Student Chapter support at Colleges and Universities
9. Scholarship programs
10. Comprehensive member and employee safety services including onsite safety training through *"Project Safe Site Plus"* and grant funded programs like "Interactive Construction Safety Training" available to all construction contractors in Michigan.
11. The Michigan Chapter AGC has two safety vans used by the Safety Director to provide onsite training to projects in Michigan's Lower and Upper Peninsula.

Michigan Road Builders Association (MRBA)

Founded in 1928, the Michigan Road Builders Association has been the leading trade association representing the interests of private sector road and bridge contractors responsible for the vast majority of all road and bridge projects in the State of Michigan. MRBA members also include equipment and materials suppliers, attorneys and insurance agencies specializing in the construction industry, and consultants.

Member benefits include effective communication with the Michigan Department of Transportation, the promotion of pro-highway legislation both at the state and federal levels, safety training, networking and educational opportunities, and negotiating with major unions on labor agreements. MRBA's *Interchange* magazine uses timely and relevant articles to inform members on a number of diverse subjects. Strides in the area of technology have allowed MRBA to be the first to provide its membership with on-line, "As-Read" bid letting results, thus saving members valuable travel time and up-to-the-minute letting information.

MRBA consistently lobbies to retain and increase state and federal funding used to build and maintain infrastructure. The association strives to be at the forefront of all issues concerning road and bridge building, repair, and safety, and continues to regularly grow in membership. Respected by government agencies, and partnered with various industry affiliates, MRBA continues to be "The Voice of Michigan's Road and Bridge Building Industry".

PDM Bridge, LLC

PDM Bridge is a leader in the bridge fabrication industry with extensive experience in fabricating complex bridge structures. Although based in Eau Claire, Wisconsin, the firm has played an important role in some of the largest bridge construction projects in Michigan. The second Blue Water Bridge is 1,480 feet (451 meters) long and joins Port Huron, Michigan, to

of schedule. The M-6 Thornapple Bridges project in Kent County, Michigan, consisted of four bridges totaling 133 girders. PDM Bridge participated in this project as the fabricator of structural steel. In addition to these Michigan projects, the firm fabricated and erected the Gateway Arch in St. Louis, Missouri. PDM has been awarded the contract for the Woodrow

numerically controlled equipment and are capable of applying full shop coat paint systems in an environmentally controlled atmosphere. PDM Bridge resulted from the consolidation of three fabrication facilities with histories dating back to the late 1800's. Pitt-Des Moines, Inc., initiated the unification in 1994. This large 110-year-old publicly traded company merged the steel fabri-

The Blue Water Bridge

Sarnia, Ontario over the St. Clair River. PDM Bridge fabricated this three-span continuous steel tied arch bridge jointly with a Canadian firm. It was named Prize Bridge in the Long Span category for the year 2000. The U.S. 131 S-Curve project consisted of a mile long S-curve series of bridges capable of carrying 120,000 vehicles per day over the Grand River and into the city of Grand Rapids. PDM Bridge participated in the project as the structural steel fabricator, shipping 262 truckloads of steel in the course of only two months. This expedited delivery allowed the project to be opened to traffic one year ahead

Wilson Bridge in Washington, DC, which will be the world's largest bascule bridge.

With modern facilities and experienced personnel, PDM Bridge has the expertise and capacity to fabricate components for all types of bridge structures. These range from conventional steel building structures and simple steel bridges to complex steel building structures and major steel bridges with fracture critical and paint endorsements as set forth in the AISC certification program.

The PDM Bridge fabricating facilities are equipped with state-of-the-art

cation facilities of Hartwig Manufacturing, located in Wausau, Wisconsin, and Phoenix Steel, located in Eau Claire, Wisconsin. In 1997, PDM Bridge acquired its third fabrication facility, Sheffield Steel, located in Palatka, Florida. This final acquisition gave the firm the opportunity to utilize inter-coastal waterways to transport finished product to customers by barge directly from the Florida facility. Serving the economic and personal needs of our society by connecting complex transportation systems, the firm takes great pride in their products.

The Life Sciences Institute and Bio-Medical Science Research Building on the campus of The University of Michigan under construction.

Greater Michigan Plumbing and Mechanical Contractors Association (PMC)

The Greater Michigan Plumbing & Mechanical Contractors Association (PMC) was formed over 55 years ago to provide mechanical contractors with a unified voice for the industry. Along with labor relations, the Association stresses contractor services, education, and community service. The Association also promotes the educational benefits of its workers. Working in conjunction with Washtenaw Community College, apprentices with the Greater Michigan UA 190 Training Program earn an Associate's Degree while they are completing their apprenticeship program. Many workers go on to get their Bachelor's Degrees from universities such as Eastern Michigan

University.

The Association also sponsors a very active Student Chapter at Ferris State University and recently formed one at Eastern Michigan University. PMC was instrumental in helping form the local Ann Arbor Student Home Building Program that is just starting its 34th home.

Another important aspect of the PMC is the community outreach programs that they organize each year. One of the ways PMC gives back to the community is through their *Handicapped & Elderly Assistance to Service Our Neighbors* ("HEATS ON") program. As part of the program, the volunteers provide free safety inspections on

furnaces, repair heating systems and help ensure the homeowner's safety with new smoke detectors and carbon monoxide detectors. The members of the PMC also help with Miracle Flights for Kids, conducts USO fundraisers, Habitat for Humanity, Hospice as well as several other worthy causes.

Through its many commitments to coalitions and organizations throughout Michigan, PMC strives to educate the public and the construction user on utilizing responsible and professional contractors whose workers provide the best the construction industry has to offer.

Slagter Construction

Brian Slagter's grandfather, John Slagter, for many years was a general superintendent for VanderVeen Construction. When Brian's father completed four years in the Navy, he returned home to the company's first project, which was half completed. The year was 1955. Brian's grandfather and father worked side by side every day until later in the 1960's when John Slagter retired.

Initially the company built box culverts as a three-employee subcontractor for larger companies. With the advent of pre-fabricated culverts, Slagter built a few new bridges mostly in rural areas over small streams. Since 1972, the company began overlaying bridge decks with concrete or waterproof membranes.

In 1982, Slagter acquired Moored Construction, which specialized in guardrail installation. The company now focuses on every phase of bridge rehabilitation and guardrail installation and sales. Some notable projects where the rehabilitations were completed by Slagter include: Wealthy Street, Franklin Street, and Hall Street bridges over US 131 in Grand Rapids (1991), US 31 reconstruction in Muskegon (2000), and the I-496 re-construction in Lansing (2001). The company has operated as dba Slagter Construction since 1999.

Year Founded: 1955

Number of
Employees: 100

Significant Achievements:
US 31 reconstruction
in Muskegon,
I-496 Bridge and
guardrail reconstruction

President: Brian Slagter

U.S. 23 Bridges at the Huron River

Spence Brothers

Spence Brothers was founded in 1893 by brothers Hugh and Matt Spence, in response to the need to rebuild much of the East Side of Saginaw, Michigan, which had been lost in a devastating fire. The business quickly grew from a local residential contractor to a regional firm constructing commercial, religious and educational buildings. The founders and their sons dedicated their lives to developing a reputation for quality and dependability that grew throughout Michigan.

During the depression the company survived by finding and building government Post Office facilities across the eastern United States. The following decades brought tremendous growth to Spence Brothers based on their ability to tackle any project regardless of size or complexity. They constructed major educational, healthcare, commercial, industrial, recreational and governmental facilities throughout Michigan. Spence Brothers built a major share of the University of Michigan campus from Crisler Arena and the Medical Science Research Building to many classrooms, library and dormitory facilities.

Currently, Spence Brothers is led by third and fourth generation family members Douglas M. Spence, Richard W. Spence, Herbert A. Spence, III, Matthew Spence IV, Robert S. Spence III and Edwin A. Spence, III, as well as key "extended family" employees including General Superintendent, Lawrence V. Walraven, Jr. and Operations Directors Brian Keeler and Ann Curran. They have led Spence Brothers during another period of tremendous growth, doubling their sales volume over the past three years.

Spence Brothers is now an industry leader in providing Construction Management and Design/Build services for major educational, healthcare, recreational and water/wastewater facilities across Michigan. They have also kept their roots as a general contractor firmly intact, by keeping their reputation for excellent craftsmen that self-perform concrete and carpentry work. After 110 years Spence Brothers continues to provide an increasingly rare combination of professional construction services and true builders of Michigan.

Saginaw Convention Center

The Turner Construction Company

Turner Construction Company, a subsidiary of the Turner Corporation, was founded in 1902 and the firm's construction experience in Michigan dates back to 1913 with the construction of the Agricultural Chemical Company's factory in Ecorse. Based in downtown Detroit, Turner Construction prides itself on the fact that every project it has begun in its 101-year history has been completed. In Michigan, that roster includes such successful enterprises as the Vickers Company Oak Park defense Plant, which was built in 1942, and the entire town of White Pine, Michigan, which was constructed between 1952 and 1954. The Michigan office is also proud of its ISO 9001:2000 Quality Certification and the more than 120 full-time employees in Michigan who embrace the concepts of quality and continuous improvement. Recent and current projects give an idea of the broad spectrum of construction carried out by Turner Construction.

Turner provided pre-construction and construction management services for the $250 million Comerica Park project. The 40,000-seat ballpark, new home of the Detroit Tigers, features no outfield seats in its upper bowl and along the ballpark's south side, a wrought iron fence is all that stands between the sidewalk and fans outside the park. This unique design allows people on the outside to see what's happening on the inside of the ballpark while giving fans inside the park an unobstructed view of downtown Detroit. Completed in 2000, the project included a 1,000 car parking structure, 1,500 space parking lot and related infrastructure improvements.

Turner's Michigan office provided pre-construction and construction management services for a 2.4-acre polar bear exhibit and 12,000 sq. ft. amphibian center at the Detroit Zoo. The Arctic Ring of Life exhibit takes

The Artic Ring of Life at the Detroit Zoo

visitors on a virtual trek to the North Pole. Guests to the Zoo experience the tundra, open sea and pack ice of the Arctic environment, and the animals that are distinctively adapted to life there.

The $20 million Wayne State University Williams Mall Undergraduate Housing project provides an environment properly suited for more conventional animals— 370 college students. Turner provided the design-build services for the 128,000 sq. ft., six-story block and plank frame structure clad in WSU's standard brick color. The residence hall includes a 380-seat dining hall, ground floor offices, conference rooms, retail, and student apartments. The building is adjacent to the undergraduate library and is across from the Student Center and the Recreation and Fitness Center.

Two other Turner projects crucial to the rebirth of downtown Detroit involve hotels. The Hilton Garden Inn Hotel on the corner of Randolph and Gratiot is the first Detroit hotel to be built in the downtown area in over 10 years. Turner also carried out $86 million in renovations to the 1,340-room Detroit Renaissance Center Marriott Hotel. The work on the core and shell of the 73-

story landmark involved 1,223,000 sq. ft. and was done in phases over a two-to-three year period.

A $24.3 million project currently underway is the Doubletree Hotel and Conference Center in Bay City, Michigan. The hotel and conference center will reside on the east bank of the Saginaw River, enabling a spectacular view of the city. The first class facilities will include a 150-room Doubletree Hotel and attached 24,000 square foot Conference Center with a total of 310 parking places. Completion is slated for February 2004.

The Pfizer Technical Development Facility in Ann Arbor, Michigan, is a $185 million project completed in 2002. This 435,000 square foot facility includes research and development, product development, and a laboratory-office complex of two major buildings: the laboratory and office building, and the development building. The buildings bring all technical development functions closer to other R&D related functions. In addition to the buildings, the project includes a tunnel that passes below Huron Parkway to connect to the dining and meeting facilities elsewhere on the Pfizer campus.

Walbridge Aldinger Company

CORPORATE OVERVIEW

Walbridge Aldinger Company is one of Michigan's oldest and largest construction companies. Founded in 1916, the company has a long and distinguished history as part of the Michigan construction industry, growing steadily over the years to its current position as one of the top 50 construction organizations in the United States. Walbridge's expertise serves many segments of the marketplace, including automotive and industrial facilities, waste and water infrastructure programs, commercial offices and retail structures, airports, roads and bridges, and healthcare.

Success in the construction industry is based upon an organization's devotion towards providing the best construction-related services that exceed a customer's expectation. Walbridge's philosophy of continuous improvement is a vital element to our commitment to excellence and in developing the most competitive costing structures that focus on eliminating excesses and maximizing efficiency. Walbridge Aldinger Company will continue to build upon its reputation as an innovative leader in the construction industry, as we commit to servicing you as a satisfied and valued client.

Walbridge Aldinger Company is proud to be a part of the "legacy" of the Michigan Building Industry.

WALBRIDGE ALDINGER
CORPORATE HEADQUARTERS
613 Abbott Street
Detroit, MI 48226-2521
(313) 963-8000 FAX: (313) 963-8150
www.walbridge.com

ANNUAL REVENUES: Appr. $1 billion

REPRESENTATIVE QUALITIES
IS0 9001 / 2000 Certified
First ISO Certified Contractor in the United States
Safety EMR: .48
Bonding in 9 Figures

NUMBER OF EMPLOYEES: 529

John Rakolta, Jr.
Chairman & CEO

Building Michigan Sponsors

AnLaan Corporation
P.O. Box 333
Ferrysburg, MI 49406
(616) 846-8442
fax (616) 846-8761

Aristeo Construction
12811 Farmington Road
Livonia, MI 48150
(734) 427-9111
www.Aristeo.com

Associated Underground Contractors (AUC)
3413 Woodsedge Drive
Okemos, MI 48805-1640
(517) 347-8336
fax (517) 347-8344
www.aucmi.org

Blue Cross Blue Shield of Michigan
600 E. Lafayette
Detroit, MI 48226
(313) 225-8000
fax (313) 225-8403
www.BCBSM.com

Bricklayers Local 1 Michigan
International Union of Bricklayers and Allied Craftworkers (BAC)
21031 Ryan Road
Warren, MI 48091
(586) 754-0888
fax (586) 754-5889
www.bricklayers.org

C.A. Hull Co., Inc.
8177 Goldie Road
Walled Lake, MI 48390
(248) 363-3813
fax (248) 363-2399
www.cahull.com

Camps Services
3051 Thompson Road
Fenton, MI 48430
(810) 750-5600
fax (810) 750-5601
www.CampServ-SwimmingPools.com

Construction Association of Michigan (CAM)
43636 Woodward Avenue
P.O. Box 3204
Bloomfield Hills, MI 48302-3204
(248) 972-1000
fax (248) 972-1001
www.cam-online.com

Davis Construction
616 S. Creyts Road Suite A
Lansing, MI 48917
(517) 323-9900
fax (517) 323-0330
www.davisconstructionsite.com

E.C. Korneffel
2691 Veterans Parkway
Trenton, MI 48183
(734) 676-2131
fax (734) 676-0788
www.korneffel.com

Echo Publications, Inc.
Tom Putters
300 E. Fourth Street
Royal Oak, MI 48067
(248) 582-9690

Graders and Landscapers Association
36700 Northline Road
Romulus, MI 48174
(313) 654-3700

Greater Detroit Building Trades Council
1640 Porter Street
Detroit, MI 48216
(313) 965-5080
fax (313) 965-3232
www.detroitbuildingtrades.org

Greater Michigan Plumbing and Mechanical Contractors Association, Inc.
58 Parkland Plaza Suite 600
Ann Arbor, MI 48103
(734) 665-4681
fax (734) 665-5051
www.greatermichiganpmc.org

International Brotherhood of Electrical Workers (IEBW)
Local Union #252
7920 Jackson Road
Ann Arbor, MI 48103
(734) 424-0978

International Masonry Institute (IMI)
Michigan Area Office
483 Little Lake Drive Suite 100
Ann Arbor, MI 48103
(734) 769-1654
fax (734) 769-6270
(800) IMI-0988
www.IMIWEB.org

International Union of Operating Engineers' Local 324
37450 Schoolcraft Suite 110
Livonia, MI 48150
(734) 462-3660
fax (734) 462-4830
www.iuoe324.org

John E. Green Company
220 Victor Avenue
Highland Park, MI 48203
(313) 868-2400
fax (313) 868-0011
www.johnegreen.com

Journeyman & Apprentice Training Fund, Inc.
Sam T. Hart Education Center
Operating Engineers Local 324 Howell Training Center
275 E. Highland Road
Howell, MI 48843
(517) 546-9610
fax (517) 546-9793
www.iuow324.org

Laborer's Local 1191
2161 West Grand Blvd.
Detroit, MI 48208
(313) 894-2241
fax (313) 894-6250

Management & Unions Serving Together (MUST)
277 Gratiot, Suite 400
Detroit, MI 48226
(313) 964-2662
fax (313) 964-5511
www.must.org

Marsh
600 Renaissance Center Suite 2100
Detroit, MI 48243
(313) 393-6800
fax (313) 393-6515
www.marsh.com

Martopia
Christi Clark
8050 Summerfield Road Suite 3
Lambertville, MI 48144
(734) 854-1800
www.martopia.com

McMahon Helicopter
8351 Ronda Drive
Canton, MI 48187
(800) 752-8590
fax (313) 459-6315
www.mcmahonhelicopters.com

Michigan CAT
28004 Center Oaks Court
Wixom, MI 48393
(248) 348-0900
fax (248) 348-3081
www.michigancat.com

Michigan Chapter Associated General Contractors (AGC)
2323 N. Larch
Lansing, MI 48906
(517) 371-1550
fax (517) 371-1131
www.mi.agc.org

Michigan Road Builders Association (MRBA)
924 Centennial Way Suite 460
Lansing, MI 48917
(517) 886-9000
fax (517) 886-8960
www.mrba.com

National Electrical Contractors Association (NECA)
Ann Arbor Division, Michigan Chapter
1026 N. Washington Ave.
Lansing, MI 48906
(517) 372-3080

PDM Bridge
2800 Melby Street
Eau Claire, WI 54703
(715) 835-2250
fax (715) 835-4244
www.pdmbridge.com

Slagter Construction
1326 142nd Avenue
Wayland, MI 49348
(616) 877-0020
fax (616) 877-0030

Stante Excavating
7440 Salem
Northville, MI 48167
(248) 380-9922

Spence Brothers
417 McCoskry Street
Saginaw, MI 48601
(989) 752-0400
fax (989) 752-8769
www.spencebrothers.com

Turner Construction
535 Griswold Suite 200
Detroit, MI 48226-3612
(313) 596-0500
fax (313) 596-4973
www.turnerconstruction.com

Walbridge Aldinger Company
613 Abbott Street
Detroit, MI 48226-2521
(313) 963-8000
www.walbridge.com

Index